THE 8 KEYS TO END BULLYING
ACTIVITY BOOK
FOR KIDS & TWEENS

This book belongs to:

_____

8 Keys to Mental Health Series
Babette Rothschild, Series Editor

The 8 Keys series of books, edited by Babette Rothschild, provides readers with brief, inexpensive, and high-quality self-help books on a variety of topics in mental health. Each volume is written by an expert in the field, someone who is capable of presenting evidence-based information in a concise and clear way. These books stand out by offering cutting-edge, relevant theory in easily digestible portions, written in an accessible style. The tone is respectful of the reader and the messages are immediately applicable. Filled with exercises and practical strategies, these books empower readers to help themselves.

THE **8** KEYS TO END BULLYING
ACTIVITY BOOK
FOR KIDS & TWEENS

WORKSHEETS, QUIZZES, GAMES, & SKILLS

FOR PUTTING THE KEYS INTO ACTION

Signe Whitson

W. W. NORTON & COMPANY

INDEPENDENT PUBLISHERS SINCE 1923

NEW YORK • LONDON

Important Note: *The 8 Keys To End Bullying Activity Book For Kids & Tweens* is intended to provide general information on the subject of health and well-being; it is not a substitute for medical or psychological treatment and may not be relied upon for purposes of diagnosing or treating any illness. Please seek out the care of a professional healthcare provider if you are pregnant, nursing, or experiencing symptoms of any potentially serious condition.

For information about permission to reproduce selections from this book, write to Permissions, W. W. Norton & Company, Inc., 500 Fifth Avenue, New York, NY 10110

For information about special discounts for bulk purchases, please contact W. W. Norton Special Sales at specialsales@wwnorton.com or 800-233-4830

Manufacturing by LSC Crawfordsville
Book design by Vicki Fischman
Production manager: Christine Critelli

Library of Congress Cataloging-in-Publication Data

ISBN: 978-0-393-71180-6 (pbk.)

W. W. Norton & Company, Inc., 500 Fifth Avenue, New York, N.Y. 10110
www.wwnorton.com

W. W. Norton & Company Ltd., 15 Carlisle Street, London W1D, 3BS

1 2 3 4 5 6 7 8 9 0

To Richard, Hannah, and Elise

and to young people everywhere
who stand up, speak out, help others,
and choose kindness always.

TABLE OF CONTENTS

ACKNOWLEDGMENTS

As I say to my students and note often in this Activity Book, *words matter*. And so it is only fitting for me to acknowledge with words my love, gratitude and admiration for the many people whose actions, experiences, stories, suggestions, wisdom and encouragement inspired me to write the *8 Keys to End Bullying* books, especially:

My daughters, Hannah and Elle, who are the most interesting people I know and whose empathy and kindness make me proud every single day. May your voices always be strong, confident, and kind and may your lives be blessed with love, laughter, hard work, and the knowledge that you make the world a better place. Thank you for being you—I love you more than mere *words* could ever say.

My husband, Richard, who has always been so encouraging of my writing and so understanding when I give him that look that says, "Shhhhhhh! I'm writing. I'll see you in a few hours." I love you and appreciate you.

My mom, Karen, who is the first real-live author I ever knew and my forever role-model of kindness, generosity, and unconditional love.

Ben Yarling at W.W. Norton, who was a champion of this Activity Book & Companion Guide from the very beginning. Your vision for what these books could be and creative suggestions all along the way were tremendously helpful. I am very grateful for your ideas and input and humbled by your belief in me. Thank you.

My students at Circle of Seasons Charter School: you have been some of my greatest teachers. What an honor it is to be your School Counselor (your Queen Signe) and to be part of your young lives. I love watching you grow and am proud of each and every one of you. Thank you for being among the first 'recipients' of many of the activities included in this Activity Book and for showing me first-hand how to make the lessons as helpful as possible to students everywhere.

Phil Arnold, the COS Board, and our amazingly supportive faculty: thank you for allowing me the time away from school that I needed to work on these books. I know that you took on extra roles in order to support our kiddos when I was not in the building and I appreciate all that you do, every day.

Nicholas Long, Frank Fecser, and my LSCI Institute colleagues around the globe: thank you for teaching me so early on in my career to always look beyond behavior and make time to genuinely understand the experiences, thoughts, and feelings that underlie the actions of young people. This framework guides all of my best work with kids. What's more, this fundamental belief in the power of relationships has led me to always persist in reaching out to kids who seem unreachable and to insist that kids who bully are worthy of more than just rote punishments and alienating labels.

Mary Kate Joseph, Kiely Ostfeld, and Kelly Richenaker: You are outstanding examples of what it takes to create cultures of kindness in classrooms. When I write about teachers who bring an end to bullying by prioritizing strong, positive connections with students, I am writing about you. When I describe professionals who infuse problem-solving, empathy-building, and social skills development into every subject they teach, I am describing you. And when I gratefully think of the difference-makers in my own daughters' lives, I am thinking of you! You are true champions of children and I am beyond lucky to know you and learn from you.

WELCOME TO YOUR ACTIVITY BOOK

Dear Readers:

My name is Signe Whitson. I am a School Counselor. Many of the students at my school call me Queen Signe. Some of them do it because they like to be silly. Others do it just for fun. But most of the students I work with use this term because, at our school, we are always talking about how *words matter.* The way we speak to each other, including the names we use and the words we choose, all affect how we feel about ourselves and how we enjoy our time at school.

I wrote this Activity Book to share with you ideas for making your school and community a kinder place. It will also help you learn skills to handle conflict and bullying. There are more than 40 Activities in this book that will teach you how to:

- tell the difference between rudeness, mean behavior, and bullying
- respond well when someone is bullying you
- stand up for someone else before, during, and after bullying
- have fun online and while texting without hurting others or putting yourself at risk
- keep a cool head and make good choices, even when you are upset
- pick fun, kind, trustworthy friends
- connect with helpful adults when you need to
- reach out to kids who bully, knowing that everyone has a story
- help others become aware of the problem of bullying

How to Use This Activity Book:

This Activity Book is meant to be useful and **fun**. There are quizzes, experiments, and questions and answers. There are also games, puzzles, writing opportunities, and real-life stories. Every part of this book is designed to teach you how to bring an end to bullying and choose kindness.

 The book is divided into 8 Keys. A *Key* is another name for a chapter. Each Key contains Activities that teach similar skills.

The 40 Activities are divided into sections:

- A few opening sentences tell you what each Activity will be about.
- A THINK ABOUT IT section in each Activity teaches you ways to stop bullying. Sometimes this section will feature real-life stories of kids who have been through bullying. Other times, you will be asked to share about your own life.
- Several Activities have a WRITE ABOUT IT section. Here you can express yourself through a journal.
- Some Activities include a MORE TO THINK ABOUT section. It will challenge you to take your learning to the next level.
- A few of the Activities even include a **BONUS** section. This is where you can add points to a quiz score or go the extra mile to make your learning really last.

In this Activity Book, you'll also find other fun things:

- At the end of each Key is a CHECKPOINT. CHECKPOINTS give you the chance to think back on all that you have learned in the Key. They help to make sure you understand each main point. Then you can move on to the next part of the Activity Book!

- After you complete each CHECKPOINT, you will earn a **KEY** for that section. Color in each Key to show that you have completed all the Activities. You have unlocked the skills you need to bring an end to bullying!
- Once you have collected all 8 Keys, you will find your very own **CERTIFICATE OF ACHIEVEMENT**. Fill it out with your name. Hang it up proudly to celebrate all your hard work!
- At the very end of your Activity Book are several pages that are JUST FOR YOU. Here you can journal, draw, and collect your thoughts. These pages can help you work through challenging situations. This is also a place to celebrate the times when you handle conflicts really well!

You may choose to complete the Activities in order. Or, you may decide to skip around, depending on your interests. Use the checkboxes in the Table of Contents to keep track of each Activity as you finish it. You can also use this section to look ahead to all the Activities still to come!

You may work on your own, or you may complete the Activities with kids from your class, school, troop, or other group. You are encouraged to talk about your learning and ideas with your parents and friends. *Practicing new skills on real people is the best way to get good at stopping bullying.* As long as you are thinking, learning, and enjoying yourself, there is no wrong way to use this Activity Book.

Have fun, be strong, and choose kindness always!

(Queen) Signe

KNOW THE BASICS OF BULLYING

ACTIVITY 1: WHAT IS BULLYING?

ON JUST ABOUT ANY DAY IN ANY SCHOOL, you can hear a teacher warn a student against bullying. Just as often, you might hear a kid accuse a classmate of being a bully. It's a great thing when adults and kids work together to stop cruelty. But there may be days when you—and your teachers—get tired of hearing the word "bully." You might even stop taking the word seriously.

But *not* paying attention to bullying is dangerous for everyone! That's why, before we do anything else in this book, we need to agree on what bullying is . . . and what bullying is not.

THINK ABOUT IT

Children's author Trudy Ludwig (2013)* uses these definitions:

Rude = Accidentally saying or doing something hurtful.

Mean = Saying or doing something to hurt a person on purpose, once or maybe twice.

Bullying = Cruel behavior, done on purpose and repeated over time, that involves an imbalance of power.

Rude = Accidentally saying or doing something hurtful.

Rude behaviors include:

- Burping out loud
- Butting in line
- Bragging about making a team
- Stepping on someone's foot by accident

Rude behaviors are usually thoughtless and ill-mannered, but they are not meant to hurt anyone.

* Ludwig, T. (2013, February 20). How to talk to your kids about bullying [Blog post]. Retrieved from http://www.aplatformforgood.org/blog/entry/how-to-talk-to-your-kids-about-bullying

LIST 3 OR 4 EXAMPLES OF RUDE BEHAVIORS YOU HAVE SEEN:

_____   _____

_____   _____

Mean = Saying or doing something to hurt a person on purpose, once or maybe twice.

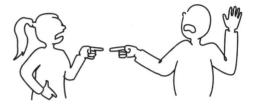

The main difference between "rude" and "mean" behavior is that rudeness is not usually planned. Mean behavior, on the other hand, is done on purpose.

Mean behaviors include:

- Making fun of what someone looks like or what they are wearing
  - Saying, "I don't like your short hair. You look like a boy."
  - Saying, "Gross. Why did you wear that dress?"
- Insulting someone's intelligence or ability
  - Saying, "You're so stupid."
  - Saying, "You stink at soccer."
- Saying or doing something unkind after a fight with a friend
  - Saying, "I hate you."
  - Taking something that doesn't belong to you.

Make no mistake: Mean behaviors are very hurtful and should be avoided at all times! Still, being mean is different from bullying. We'll talk about that next.

LIST 3 OR 4 EXAMPLES OF MEAN BEHAVIORS YOU HAVE SEEN:

_____   _____

_____   _____

Kids who bully say or do something hurtful to others on purpose. They keep doing it again and again with no sense of guilt or shame. Kids who bully have more power than the kids they pick on. This power may come from being older, stronger, or bigger. It may also come from getting several kids to gang up on one target so that the target feels hurt and alone.

Bullying = Cruel behavior, done on purpose and repeated over time, that involves an imbalance of power.

KEY POINT

To understand bullying, remember the 3 P's:

1. It is done on **P**urpose. There is nothing "accidental" or unplanned about bullying.
2. It is a **P**attern. The cruelty happens over and over again.
3. It is all about **P**ower. The cruel person has more control and influence than the target.

EXAMPLE OF BULLYING:

Tatum sits next to Haley in class. Haley is very smart. She is quiet, but kind to everyone. Haley has food allergies. She is very careful when it comes to eating treats during class parties.

Tatum thinks it's cool to make fun of Haley in front of everyone else. Every time they get back a test, she yells out Haley's grade to the whole class. Instead of feeling proud, Haley feels embarrassed because of the mean voice Tatum uses. She asks Tatum to stop, but Tatum laughs in her face and says, "Or what, nerd?" All the kids laugh when Tatum says this. Haley wants to cry.

For her birthday, Tatum brings in peanut butter brownies. Tatum knows that Haley is allergic to peanuts and would need to go to the hospital if she ever ate one. Still, Tatum puts the plate of peanut butter brownies on Haley's desk. She gets the whole class to tell Haley that she has to eat one to be polite. All the kids start saying, "Eat one! Eat one! Eat one!" Haley doesn't know what to do. She runs out of the room.

LIST 2 EXAMPLES OF BULLYING YOU HAVE SEEN:

1. _____

2. _____

Why Do I Need to Know the Difference Between Being Rude, Being Mean, and Bullying?

It is important to know the difference between rude, mean, and bullying behavior so that you understand what you are dealing with and know how to respond. The skills in this Activity Book will help you know **what to say** and **what to do** anytime you see bullying. You will gain the *confidence* and *power* you need to help bring an end to bullying.

In the next Activity, you will read about situations that happened to young people in real life. You will then figure out if they are acts of rudeness, meanness, or bullying.

ACTIVITY 2: IS IT RUDE, IS IT MEAN, OR IS IT BULLYING?

IN THE LAST ACTIVITY, you learned the difference between being rude, being mean, and bullying. One goal of this Activity Book is to teach you how to handle rude and mean behavior on your own. You will also learn **how** and **when** to ask for an adult's help to deal with bullying.

THINK ABOUT IT

Directions:

For each of the situations below, decide if the behavior is rude, mean, or bullying. Circle the BEST response. (*Correct answers are found on the last page of the Activity.*)

EXAMPLE:

Kayla tells MacKenzie that she can't sit with her on the bus today. Kayla says she is saving the seat for someone else.

(Rude)   Mean   Bullying

1. Lucas is in a bad mood. He tells Damien that he is the worst player in the whole grade. He says Damien can't play soccer at recess.

Rude   Mean   Bullying

2. Katie always bosses Talia around. On Friday, Talia makes plans to go to the school dance with her new friend, Gwen. Katie tells Talia that if she hangs out at the dance with Gwen, everyone will think she is a total weirdo and no one will like her anymore. At lunch, Katie tells everyone that it would be a really funny joke to all laugh out loud when Talia gets there.

Rude   Mean   Bullying

3. Kevin and David are close friends. In school, they have a fight. Kevin calls David a name and David shoves him.

Rude   Mean   Bullying

4. Maggie keeps making fun of Jessie for hanging out with boys and wearing long basketball shorts to school every day. In gym, Maggie tells Jessie to play on the boys' team. In math, she writes the words "You're so gay" on Jessie's desk.

Rude   Mean   Bullying

5. Madelyn won't talk to Ella. When Ella asks her what is wrong, Madelyn says, "Figure it out!" She gives Ella dirty looks when they pass each other in the hall. Ella tries to find out from Madelyn's friends what the problem is. They will not talk to Ella. For 2 weeks, Ella is left out at lunch and blocked from group texts.

Rude   Mean   Bullying

6. Brady tells JP he will beat him up if he touches his cars. He then shoves JP out of his way. During math, he throws a spitball at JP. He also kicks JP's chair out from under him. He tells JP he will punch him in the face if JP tells the teacher.

Rude   Mean   Bullying

7. Olivia thinks that Lily and Ariana are becoming close friends. She worries that she will be left out. She is nice to Ariana at school, but she is always insulting her online. Last night, she texted a rumor about Ariana to the whole class.

Rude   Mean   Bullying

8. Maeve and Kristy are playing a game. Tasha walks over to them. Maeve and Kristy look up briefly and smile. Then they go right back to their game. Tasha feels left out. She yells at the other girls for ignoring her.

Rude   Mean   Bullying

9. Kaitlyn and Gabby are best friends. In school, they have a fight. Gabby calls Kaitlyn a name, and Kaitlyn deletes Gabby from an online "friends" list. The next day, they make up and are friends again.

Rude   Mean   Bullying

THINK ABOUT IT

EXAMPLE:

Kayla & MacKenzie: Kayla is being **rude**. Although saving a seat for someone else is okay, Kayla could have offered MacKenzie a seat close by. She could have made plans to sit together another day. This would keep MacKenzie's feelings from getting hurt. There is no evidence that Kayla was being mean on *purpose*. It doesn't sound like this is a *pattern*. Kayla is not abusing *power* by getting others to gang up on MacKenzie.

1. Lucas & Damien: Lucas is being **mean**. His bad mood causes him to say cruel words on *purpose*. There is no evidence of a *pattern* of cruel behavior. There is no *power* difference.

2. Talia & Katie: Katie is acting like a **bully**. She uses *power* unfairly to get the girls at the lunch table to laugh at Talia. She also uses words like "everyone" and "no one" on *purpose* to threaten Talia about how she will be left out if she does not do what Katie wants her to do. Since Katie is always bossing Talia around, we know this is a *pattern* of how she treats Talia.

3. David & Kevin: Kevin and David are being **rude** to each other. This is not bullying. Because the boys are usually friends, their *power* is about equal.

4. Maggie & Jessie: Maggie is acting like a **bully**. She makes fun of Jessie over and over again, so this is a *pattern*. She tries to hurt her feelings on *purpose*. It is

never okay to call people names based on how they dress or what they look like. The word "gay" should never, ever be used as a put-down.

5. <u>Madelyn & Ella:</u> Madelyn is acting like a **bully**. She is using her friendship as a weapon to hurt Ella. She is also getting her friends involved, which gives her more *power*. Ella is left feeling all alone. It would be most helpful for Madelyn to talk to Ella about the reason she is upset. The other girls should refuse to block Ella from their texting.

6. <u>Brady & JP:</u> Brady is acting like a **bully**. He shows a *pattern* of cruel actions that hurt JP on *purpose*. Brady is using threats to make himself seem more *powerful* than JP.

7. <u>Olivia, Lily, & Ariana:</u> Olivia is acting like a **bully**. She is afraid that Lily and Ariana are going to become better friends with each other than they are with her. She hasn't learned yet that friendship is not a competition. Instead of being kind and trying to become better friends with the girls, she chooses to hurt Ariana with online insults and rumors.

8. <u>Maeve, Kristy, & Tasha:</u> Maeve and Kristy are playing a game when Tasha gets there. When Tasha arrives, they smile at her but do not stop their game. Maeve and Kristy show **rude** behavior by not talking to Tasha. However, there is no evidence that this is done on *purpose* to hurt Tasha's feelings. When Tasha yells at Maeve and Kristy, she makes the problem worse. Tasha should have stayed calm. She should have told the girls that she wanted to hang out with them when their game was over.

9. Kaitlyn & Gabby: Every friendship has bumps in the road. Even BFFs do not agree all the time. A real, healthy friendship can handle arguments. It can even handle anger from time to time. We know that Kaitlyn and Gabby made up quickly. Therefore, this is an example of **mean** behavior.

Mean behavior can turn into drama between girls when other friends get involved, take sides, and start to gossip. **Whenever you can, keep a cool head. Do not add fuel to someone else's fight.** Also, be sure to tell others not to make a bad situation worse.

ACTIVITY 3: WHAT DOES BULLYING LOOK LIKE?

IN THE FIRST 2 ACTIVITIES, you learned that bullying has 3 key parts: <u>P</u>urpose, <u>P</u>attern, and <u>P</u>ower. In this Activity, you will learn the 4 most common types of bullying. You will then list the ways you see them happening in your life.

THINK ABOUT IT

Bullying may be **physical**. It may be **verbal** or **relational**. If it happens through the phone or Internet, it is **cyberbullying**.

- **Physical bullying:** This kind of bullying happens when one person tries to harm another person's body.

CAN YOU LIST AT LEAST 3 EXAMPLES OF PHYSICAL BULLYING?

EXAMPLE:

Cara always shoves Sean in line.

_____

_____   _____

_____   _____

- **Verbal bullying:** Some people say that "words will never hurt you." However, anyone who has received verbal bullying knows that cruel words and scary threats are very painful.

PUT A CHECK MARK NEXT TO THE 3 EXAMPLES OF VERBAL BULLYING.
(Answers are found at the end of this Activity.)

☐ Kicking someone's chair   ☐ Threatening to punch someone

☐ Calling someone a name   ☐ Taunting someone about their shoes

☐ Pulling someone's hair   ☐ Posting photos of someone online.

- **Relational bullying:** In relational bullying, kids use friendship—and the threat of taking their friendship away—to hurt others. This is the type of bullying most often called "drama." Because it often happens between kids who were once friends, drama can be very confusing and hurtful.

CAN YOU LIST AT LEAST 3 EXAMPLES OF RELATIONAL BULLYING?

EXAMPLE:

Erin gives Rachel the silent treatment

_____   _____

_____   _____

- **Cyberbullying:** This kind of bullying has to do with technology. It may be done using a smartphone, a tablet, social media (like Facebook or Instagram), or the Internet. As you will see in later Activities, cyberbullying can be especially bad. This is because cruel messages can spread to many people very quickly.

CIRCLE THE 2 EXAMPLES OF CYBERBULLYING.
(Answers are found on the next page.)

Jessie texts all the girls in her class that Aimee never takes a shower.

Kim passes a note to Jackson telling him she likes him.

Tim posts a photo online of an elephant next to a photo of his classmate, Rhea. He captions it, "Twins!"

Becca tells everyone not to pick Skylar to be on the softball team.

Jason takes Ben's tablet out of his backpack and smashes it on the ground.

THINK ABOUT IT

ANSWER KEY

PUT A CHECK MARK NEXT TO THE 3 EXAMPLES OF VERBAL BULLYING:

☐ Kicking someone's chair

✓ Threatening to punch someone

✓ Calling someone a name

✓ Tauntng someone about their shoes

☐ Pulling someone's hair

☐ Posting photos of someone online

CIRCLE THE 2 EXAMPLES OF CYBERBULLYING:

Jessie texts all the girls in her class that Aimee never takes a shower.

Kim passes a note to Jackson telling him she likes him.

Tim posts a photo online of an elephant next to a photo of his classmate, Rhea. He captions it, "Twins!"

Becca tells everyone not to pick Skylar to be on the softball team.

Jason takes Ben's tablet out of his backpack and smashes it on the ground

ACTIVITY 4: FOUR TYPES OF BULLYING

IN ACTIVITY 3, you learned about 4 types of bullying (physical, verbal, relational, and cyber-bullying). In this Activity, you will read a list of common bullying behaviors among kids your age. Some of these might appear on the lists you made in Activity 3. Some may be new to you. Being able to spot bullying as it occurs will help you know how to best respond.

THINK ABOUT IT

Directions:

First, circle the behaviors in the list below that you have observed or been involved in. Later, share this list with your parents and teachers. This will let them know the kinds of things happening among kids your age.

Typical Bullying Behaviors

Hitting	Tripping
Cursing	Elbowing
Posting cruel comments online	Posting party photos online to show who was NOT invited to the party
Giving the silent treatment	Talking about plans in front of people who are not included
Kicking	
Pushing	Teasing

Calling names

Threatening

Starting rumors online

Setting up a fake social media account

Spitting

Talking behind someone's back

Telling everyone to ignore someone

Altering someone's profile photo in a cruel way

Making fun of someone in a group chat

Insulting

Gossiping

Leaving someone out at lunch on purpose

Saying something cruel on purpose, then saying "Just joking"

Not allowing someone to sit with the group on the bus

Now, put each behavior from the list above into the correct category below. Bookmark this page in your Activity Book. It can be a handy guide to common bullying behaviors.

PHYSICAL BULLYING

1. Hitting

VERBAL BULLYING

1. Cursing

RELATIONAL BULLYING

1. Giving the silent treatment

CYBERBULLYING

1. Posting cruel comments online

WRITE ABOUT IT

What type of bullying do you see most often? Which type of bullying is most painful for you?
Write about a time when you were bullied in this way. Tell how you handled the situation.

_____

_____

_____

_____

_____

_____

_____

_____

_____

_____

_____

_____

_____

_____

_____

_____

_____

_____

_____

_____

Typical Bullying Behaviors
A N S W E R   K E Y

PHYSICAL BULLYING

Hitting

Kicking

Pushing

Tripping

Elbowing

Spitting

VERBAL BULLYING

Cursing

Insulting

Teasing

Calling names

Threatening

Talking behind someone's back

RELATIONAL BULLYING

Giving the silent treatment

Gossiping

Leaving someone out at lunch
 on purpose

Saying something cruel on purpose,
 then saying "Just joking"

Telling everyone to ignore someone

Not allowing someone to sit with the
 group on the bus

CYBERBULLYING

Posting party photos online to show
 who was NOT invited to the party

Posting cruel comments online

Starting rumors online

Setting up a fake social media account

Altering someone's profile photo in a
 cruel way

Making fun of someone in a group chat

ACTIVITY 5: QUIZ TIME
WHAT'S YOUR BULLY-BUSTING SPIRIT ANIMAL?

IN THE LAST ACTIVITY, you identified bullying behaviors that you have seen or been involved in. Then you wrote about the type of bullying that you find most painful. In this Activity, you'll find your Bully-Busting Spirit Animal. This will help you make the best choices to respond to bullying.

THINK ABOUT IT

We all have *choices* about how to respond to bullying. Read each real-life situation from the **What's Your Bully-Busting Spirit Animal** quiz below. Then choose the response(s) you think would be best for stopping the bullying. You may choose more than one option for each situation. At the end of the quiz, we'll review your answers and talk about the best ways to stop all types of bullying.

What's Your Bully-Busting Spirit Animal?

1. Krystal and Shonnell sit together on the bus to school. Krystal is angry at Shonnell for being too noisy. She calls her "ugly" and says, "If you keep being so loud, I'm going to spit on you."

   What do you think Shonnell should do?
   A. Say, "If you spit on me, I'll punch you in the face."
   B. Turn the other way and start talking to a nice kid in the next seat.

C. Think to herself, "I like the way I look. I'm going to keep my cool and not react to what Krystal just said."

D. Change the subject. Ask Krystal if she saw that funny episode of their favorite TV show last night.

E. Look Krystal in the eye. In a strong, steady voice, say, "That's gross. Don't say that."

2. Ricky likes to be in charge of everything in his neighborhood. When Preston gets to be team captain, Ricky gets mad. He picks up a dodgeball and throws it at Preston's head.

What do you think Preston should do?
A. Grab the ball and throw it at Ricky's face as hard as he can.
B. Look at his watch and tell the other kids that he has to be home for soccer practice. Then walk home to tell his parents what happened.
C. Count to 10 to give himself time to think about what to do.
D. Try to make the crowd laugh by falling to the ground and holding his head as if it were broken in 2 pieces.
E. Say, "That would've been a great shot—if the game had started yet, Ricky. Since it didn't, chill out."

3. Elizabeth tells Tina, "If you play with Jennie today, you can't be my friend." Tina ignores Elizabeth's threat and plays with Jennie during recess. At the end of the school day, Elizabeth tells 3 other girls that tomorrow is "Don't Talk to Tina Day." They all agree to ignore Tina in school all day long.

What do you think Tina should do?

A. Start a rumor about Elizabeth. Tell everyone that she has a crush on a classmate named Carlos and only changes her underwear once a week.

B. Spend time with other friends from the class. Act as if she isn't at all bothered by what Elizabeth and the other 3 girls are doing.

C. Remind herself that she is a great kid and a great friend. Remember that her mother always tells her to focus on friends that make her feel happy.

D. When she and Elizabeth are standing close together at their cubbies, say aloud, "It sure has been a quiet day. I really needed the quiet time today. Thanks!"

E. In a calm voice, say, "I guess you're mad that I played with Jennie and that's why you and the girls aren't talking to me today. I get it."

4. Jason takes a picture of Kenny in the locker room when he is changing for football practice. He posts it online without Kenny's permission. Most of the kids in their 5th-grade class see the picture of Kenny in his underwear.

What do you think Kenny should do?

A. Text all the girls in their grade an embarrassing photo of Jason pretending to kiss a Barbie doll.

B. Take a screen shot of the post. Show it to the school counselor and ask for her help.

C. Say to himself, "I know what to do in this situation. I can handle this problem."

D. Avoid going online for a few days until the situation is fixed.

E. Say to Jason, "That's so not cool. Delete the photo online and from your phone right now."

5. Morgan and Elsa are on the same soccer team. Elsa does not treat Morgan like a teammate. She points out Morgan's mistakes and laughs at her when she falls down. In one game, Morgan misses a shot on goal. Elsa groans loudly and shouts, "Again, Morgan? Have you scored at all this season? How did you even make the team, anyway?"

What do you think Morgan should do?

A. Next time she has the ball, kick it right at Elsa's head. Then, when the referee isn't watching, trip Elsa on purpose so that she falls flat on her face during the game.

B. Stay focused on the game at the moment. Talk to the coach after the game and get his help in handling Elsa's put-downs.

C. Remind herself that she is a great soccer player, a fantastic teammate, and someone who never gives up.

D. Take a deep breath. Think about where the other team's goalie will likely punt the ball. Encourage her teammates to pass to each other.

E. Say, "Knock it off, Elsa. We're a team, remember?"

Bully-Busting Quiz Choices

Look back on the answers you chose for each of the five situations above.

If you chose mostly A's, your Spirit Animal is the Tiger. Your first thought in a conflict or bullying situation may be to attack. Like a tiger, you pounce on anyone who wrongs you. You feel strong and satisfied when you get revenge. The problem is that when you copy the behavior of someone

who bullies, you make yourself look bad in the long run. When you meet violence with violence, bad things will continue to happen over and over again.

Instead of making your situation worse, consider the following better choices:

- Reach out to trustworthy friends and adults for protection
- Use positive messages to keep yourself strong
- Change the subject
- Walk away
- Use humor
- Stand up for yourself with strong words

You'll learn more about these helpful responses to bullying in the descriptions below and throughout your Activity Book!

If you chose mostly B's, your Spirit Animal is the Wolf.

Wolves are known as pack animals because they stick close together for protection and comfort. When bullying happens, you know that connecting with friends, family members, teachers, counselors, and other helping adults gives you the protection you need. Never be afraid to reach out to your pack and tell them what is going on in your life. Connecting with others is a sign of your smarts, your strength, and your courage!

If you chose mostly C's, your Spirit Animal is the Owl.

Like the owl, you are wise and have a strong mind. The positive messages that you repeat in your head (things like "I like the way I look" and "I can handle this") give you the confidence and power you need to cope with bullying. You are smart enough to choose your friends wisely and surround yourself with people that make you feel good about yourself.

If you chose mostly D's, your Spirit Animal is the Butterfly.

Just as the caterpillar changes into a butterfly, you are wise enough to know that in a bullying situation you can:

- change the subject of the conversation
- change the scene by walking away
- change a negative into a positive
- change your focus to the task at hand
- change the tone of the conversation from anger to humor

If you chose mostly E's, your Spirit Animal is the Giraffe.

I'll bet you're wondering what having a long neck has to do with handling bullying. Good question. Just as the tall giraffe doesn't need to stretch to reach the trees, you know that you do not need to stretch the truth. You are known for being honest and a straight shooter. You tell it like it is to anyone who bullies you. Like the giraffe, you speak the straight-up truth *without being hurtful* in the process. Keep on standing tall and speaking up for yourself in proud ways! You are a role model to those around you.

If you chose a mix of options, you have the Spirit of the Zookeeper.

You know many helpful ways to stop bullying. You are smart enough to choose the best one in any situation. Being flexible like that is great! It tells others that your confidence can't be shaken. You are strong enough to make great choices to stop all types of bullying. Just be sure to steer clear of hurtful or violent acts at all times, no matter how tempting they may be in the moment.

What Is Your Bully-Busting Spirit Animal?

WHAT DID THE QUIZ SAY YOUR SPIRIT ANIMAL IS?

_____

WHAT WOULD BE YOUR IDEAL SPIRIT ANIMAL?

_____

THINK ABOUT WAYS YOU MIGHT IMPROVE OR CHANGE YOUR BULLY-BUSTING STYLE. THEN DRAW A PICTURE OF YOUR IDEAL BULLY-BUSTING SPIRIT ANIMAL BELOW:

Key 1: Bullying Basics

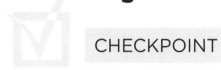

CHECKPOINT

Directions:

Before moving on to the next Key, answer the checkpoint questions below to see how much you have learned!

1. Draw a line between the type of behavior and its definition:

   Rude   Saying or doing something hurtful on purpose, once.
   Mean   Using **P**urpose, **P**attern, and **P**ower to hurt someone.
   Bullying   Saying or doing something hurtful by accident.

2. List the 4 types of bullying:

   _____   _____

   _____   _____

3. Fill in the blanks with 1 of the 4 types of bullying:

   a. Kicking and shoving are examples of _____ bullying.

   b. Leaving kids out on purpose and starting rumors about them are examples of _____ bullying.

4. Which of the following is a danger of the way a TIGER responds to bullying?

   a. When violence is met with violence, bad things happen.

   b. The bullying usually comes to a quick end.

   c. The conversation changes from anger to humor.

Key I: Bullying Basics

✓ CHECKPOINT

A N S W E R   K E Y

1. Draw a line between the type of behavior and its definition:

Rude — Saying or doing something hurtful on purpose, once.

Mean — Using **P**urpose, **P**attern, and **P**ower to hurt someone.

Bullying — Saying or doing something hurtful by accident.

2. List the 4 types of bullying:

Physical   *Relational*

Verbal   *Cyber*

3. Fill in the blanks with 1 of the 4 types of bullying:

   a. Kicking and shoving are examples of ___*physical*___ bullying.

   b. Leaving kids out on purpose and starting rumors about them are
   examples of ___*relational*___ bullying.

4. Which of the following is a danger of the way a TIGER responds to bullying?

   (**a.**) When violence is met with violence, bad things happen.

   b. The bullying usually comes to a quick end.

   c. The conversation changes from anger to humor.

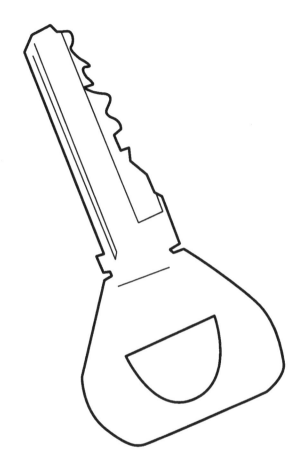

KEY 1: *I know the basics of bullying!*

2

CONNECT WITH PEOPLE YOU TRUST

ACTIVITY 6: IS IT TATTLING OR IS IT TELLING?

IN THE FIRST 2 ACTIVITIES, you read about the 3 P's of bullying. You learned that kids who bully try to make others feel **P**owerless. In Activity 5, you learned that one of the best ways for a kid to hold on to her or his power is to connect with others—just as a Wolf relies on the strength of his pack.

Do you ever worry that you will be called a tattletale if you tell an adult about a bullying situation? Guess what? *That is exactly what someone who bullies wants you to think!* One of the ways a bully takes your **P**ower is by making you too afraid and ashamed to talk to an adult.

In this Activity, you'll learn 6 rules to help you know the difference between being a TATTLE-TALE and being brave and powerful enough to TELL adults when their help is needed.

THINK ABOUT IT

Lots of kids don't know the difference between tattling and telling. This can be dangerous. It can keep important information from being shared. Parents, teachers, counselors, and other **adults can't help with a problem unless they know about it. It's your job to know when to tell them.**

On the next page are **6 SIMPLE RULES** about the difference between tattling and telling. Carefully tear the page out of your Activity Book. Tuck it into your binder at school or post it on your refrigerator at home. The better you know the **6 SIMPLE RULES**, the easier it will be for you to make the right decision.

Tattling or Telling?
6 SIMPLE RULES

IT'S TATTLING IF	IT'S TELLING IF
1. No one is hurt or injured.	**1.** Someone is hurt and needs help.
2. The person did it by accident and is sorry.	**2.** The person did it on **P**urpose to be mean.
3. This is the first time something like this has happened.	**3.** There is a **P**attern to what is going on. Nothing you have done has stopped it.
4. You have the power to solve this on your own.	**4.** You don't have the **P**ower to solve this without an adult's help.
5. Your goal is to get someone in trouble.	**5.** Your goal is to keep someone safe.
6. It's a "So what?" problem.	**6.** It's a "This matters!" problem.

USE THIS FREE SPACE TO DRAW A SITUATION ABOUT WHICH A KID SHOULD DEFINITELY TELL AN ADULT

USING THE *6 SIMPLE RULES*

Directions:

Read the following questions. Write down your answers in the space provided. Talk over your thoughts with an adult you can trust.

1. Now that you know the difference between tattling and telling:

   a. Tell about a time when you or someone you know TATTLED.

   _____

   _____

   b. Tell about a time when you or someone you know made the smart decision to TELL an adult about a bullying situation:

   _____

   _____

2. Read the 2 situations below. In the space provided, write down whether you think the situation is a "So What?" problem or a "This Matters!" problem.

Situation 1:

Jonathan and Missy are chasing each other on the playground at recess. Missy gets tired. She tells Jonathan she doesn't want to play anymore. Jonathan still wants to play. He asks Missy, "What are you, a sissy?" He gets all the boys to yell, "Missy is a sissy! Missy is a sissy!" Missy gets so mad that she starts chasing Jonathan. When she catches him, she punches him in the stomach. She says, "Would a sissy hit like that?" Jonathan's holds his stomach and whispers, "I can't breathe!"

This is a _____ problem that needs an adult's help.

Situation 2:

Jonathan and Missy are chasing each other on the playground at recess. Missy gets tired. She tells Jonathan she doesn't want to play anymore. Jonathan still wants to play. He asks Missy, "What are you, a sissy?" Missy looks Jonathan in the eye. She says, "I'm not a sissy, but I do need to catch my breath for a minute. I'll tell you when I'm ready to play again."

This is a _____ problem that the kids have worked out on their own.

ACTIVITY 7: TATTLING OR TELLING?
6 SIMPLE RULES

NOW THAT YOU UNDERSTAND the difference between tattling and telling, it's time to think about how the rules can be used in your life every day. Thinking through common, real-life situations ahead of time will help you know what to do when bullying happens.

THINK ABOUT IT

In the activity on pages 42–43, you'll use the *6 Simple Rules* to tell the difference between TATTLING and TELLING situations.

Materials Needed:

- 1 red crayon or pencil

- 1 green crayon or pencil

- A copy of **Tattling or Telling? 6 Simple Rules**

Tattling or Telling?

Directions:

Read each statement below. Each is something that a young person might say to an adult. If you think the situation is an example of tattling, color it **red**. If you think it is an example of telling, color it **green**.

Jessica just picked her nose.

Olivia won't share the jump rope with me.

Ella keeps locking Jennie in the bathroom.

Sasha butted in front of me in line.

Lily copied Brady's homework.

Kevin said I was the slowest runner in the whole 4th grade.

Dylan is bragging that he's the best reader in the whole class.

Sophie told all the girls not to play with Caitlyn at recess.

Those three 5th-grade girls keep calling Carlos a baby when he walks by.

Ainsleigh grabbed Ava's test paper. She held it up so everyone could see Ava got 10 questions wrong.

Nicole started a text rumor that Katrina and Ethan kissed. She sent it to the whole class!

Connor is throwing rocks at the girls on the swings.

Elijah trips Ariana every day when she's trying to get off the bus.

Colin deleted the characters on my video game by accident.

Fiona promised she would play with me at recess, but now she's playing with other people.

Kelly got hit in the head with a dodgeball. Now she says she feels dizzy.

Tattling or Telling?

6 Simple Rules

A N S W E R   K E Y

TATTLING BEHAVIORS (These behaviors should be shaded red on page 42–43 of your book.)	TELLING BEHAVIORS (These behaviors should be shaded green on page 42–43 of your book.)
Jessica just picked her nose.	Ella keeps locking Jennie in the bathroom.
Olivia won't share the jump rope with me.	Sophie told all the girls not to play with Caitlyn at recess.
Kevin said I was the slowest runner in the whole 4th grade.	Elijah trips Ariana every day when she's trying to get off the bus.
Sasha butted in front of me in line.	Connor is throwing rocks at the girls on the swings.
Lily copied Brady's homework.	Those three 5th-grade girls keep calling Carlos a baby when he walks by.
Dylan is bragging that he's the best reader in the whole class.	Nicole started a text rumor that Katrina and Ethan kissed. She sent it to the whole class!
Fiona promised she would play with me at recess, but now she's playing with other people.	Kelly got hit in the head with a dodgeball. Now she says she feels dizzy.
Colin deleted the characters on my video game by accident.	Ainsleigh grabbed Ava's test paper. She held it up so everyone could see Ava got 10 questions wrong.

Some of your responses may not match the ones in the Answer Key. Don't mark them wrong! Instead, talk with a helpful adult about the *6 Simple Rules*. Explain why you chose red or green for each one. Talking about the *6 Simple Rules* with others is one of the best ways to learn and understand them.

IN THE SPACE BELOW, write 1 example of tattling and 1 example of telling. Challenge a brother, sister, friend, parent, teacher, or other adult to identify your examples. Have them use the *6 Simple Rules* as a guide!

_____

_____

_____

_____

_____

_____

_____

_____

_____

_____

_____

ACTIVITY 8: WHO CAN YOU TALK TO ABOUT BULLYING?

NOW YOU KNOW THE DIFFERENCE between tattling and telling. You know when to get help for handling a bullying situation. Your next question is, *who* should you tell?

In this Activity, you will make a **Safety Plan**. It will prepare you to know <u>who</u> to talk to and <u>what</u> to say when you see bullying happen. You'll see <u>why</u> picking the right time is important. You will also learn <u>how</u> to remain *anonymous* when reporting bullying. (*Anonymous* means you tell what happened without sharing your name.)

THINK ABOUT IT

By now, you know that asking for help when you see bullying is never a sign of weakness. Connecting with others is one of the most powerful and brave things you can do. This next activity gives you the chance to make a **Safety Plan**. This plan will help you be prepared if you are involved in or find out about bullying.

KEY POINT

Some kids think that grown-ups won't do anything to stop bullying. Why should they even tell them about it? The truth, though, is that adults can't do anything if they don't know there is a problem. So make it your job to let them know!

INSTRUCTIONS FOR COMPLETING THE **SAFETY PLAN**:

QUESTION 1 asks you to list 3 adults that would help you handle a bullying situation. For this part of your Safety Plan, be sure to choose grown-ups who:

✓ Are good listeners. They take their time to really hear you when you ask them for help.

✓ You trust. Avoid an adult that would tell others that you are their source of information.

✓ Will take you seriously. Look for someone who understands that bullying is way more than just "kids being kids."

✓ Are able to stop the bullying. Your favorite aunt who lives 1,000 miles away may be a great listener. She may be trustworthy and take you seriously. But if she doesn't live close enough to actually help stop the bullying, be sure to add other adults to your list.

QUESTION 2 asks you what you'll do if these adults do not end up giving you the help you need:

✓ Don't give up! Yes, there are adults who don't pay attention to reports of bullying. Sadly, some adults get so busy with other things that they forget all about your report. But there are even more adults who care about you and want to keep you safe. *Keep talking until you find your champion who will help you!*

✓ Talk to your parents. Consider all your teachers, including teachers for Art, Music, Gym, and Music. Go to your School Counselor. Go to the principal. Go to your bus driver. Go to a coach or a youth group leader outside of school. Keep at it until you find someone who will believe you and truly help.

QUESTION 3 asks you to focus on the most important details of the bullying.

✓ Keep in mind that bullying will bring up lots of strong *feelings* in you. To really help change a situation, an adult will need to know the *facts* of what is going on. Try to keep your feelings under control.

✓ In the "What happened?" section, try to list the events in the order they happened. Include as much detail as possible.

✓ Even if you, or someone you know, chose a not-so-good response to bullying, be honest in telling an adult the full story so that they can help you.

QUESTION 4 asks you to record the date(s) and time(s) of the bullying.

✓ A common mistake kids make when dealing with bullying is to ignore it and hope it will go away. Remember: Bullying is a **P**attern of behavior that does not stop by itself. In fact, it usually just gets worse and worse over time! That's why it's important to connect with an adult before someone is badly hurt.

QUESTION 5 asks you to think about how you might make an *anonymous* report about bullying.

✓ Always remember that going to an adult in school or telling your parents about bullying is a sign of strength. You are not a tattletale. You are not a crybaby. *You are smart and brave.*

✓ Some schools have anonymous reporting forms on their website. Find out if your school has this.

✓ Other schools have phone numbers kids can use to make anonymous calls or texts about bullying.

✓ Does your school have an "Information" box where kids can leave anonymous notes about bullying?

✓ Keep in mind that you can tell an adult about bullying and ask them not to use your name. When a trustworthy adult does not tell others your name, this is called a *confidential* report.

_____'s   Safety Plan

1. List 3 adults who would help you handle a bullying situation.

_____

_____

_____

2. Who else will you talk to if these adults do not take your report of bullying seriously or do not try to help you?

_____

_____

_____

3. Before telling an adult about bullying, focus on the most important details, as best as you can remember them. Write down:
Who was involved in the situation? _____
Where did the bullying take place? _____
What happened?

_____

_____

_____

4. When did the bullying happen?
Date (s): _____
Time (s): _____
Has this ever happened before? If so, when? _____

5. You can choose to tell an adult in person about the bullying, or you may include the information from Questions 3 and 4 in an anonymous or confidential report. How will you report the bullying?
☐ Tell an adult in person
☐ Use my school's anonymous website form
☐ Use my school's confidential phone number or text system
☐ Use my school's anonymous information box
☐ Other: _____

ACTIVITY 9: FINDING FUN FRIENDSHIPS

HAVE YOU EVER HEARD THE EXPRESSION, "Cast a wide net?" When you try to get to know all kinds of kids from all sorts of places, you give yourself lots of chances to make friends who like to do the same things you do. Being bullied can make you feel lonely. One of the best things you can do to protect yourself from being lonely is to surround yourself with loyal, fun, true friendships everywhere you go.

THINK ABOUT IT

Anaya is the tallest kid in the 5th grade. Every day, she gets made fun of for her long, skinny legs and huge feet. In her neighborhood, on the other hand, she is known for being a star swimmer and great teammate. Every kid from her youth group wants her to try out for basketball. Her best friend from her old neighborhood texts with her every day after school.

Maybe you know someone like Anaya. Maybe you understand just how Anaya feels because you have had a tough time making friends at school. The truth is that bullying usually has very little to do with the person being bullied and everything to do with certain people in certain groups.

The good news is that by "casting a wide net" and finding fun friendships beyond just your class in school, you can light up the dark spaces left by not-so-nice kids elsewhere. The next Activity is designed to get you thinking about your likes, strengths, hobbies, talents, and skills so that you can connect with kids who help you feel great.

30 QUESTIONS FOR KIDS

Directions:

Use these questions (and your answers to them!) to think about the types of groups you'd like to join. Exploring activities and interests that help you feel good about yourself is a key to finding fun friendships.

1. The nicest thing anyone has ever said to me is:

_____

2. When I grow up, I want to be a:

_____

3. I like to collect:

_____

4. My top 3 favorite movies are:

_____

5. My lucky number is:

_____

6. Something I've always wanted to learn to do is:

_____

7. 4 words I use to describe myself are:

_____

8. An ideal friend is someone who:

_____

9. The best app I've ever used is:

_____

10. The hardest thing I've ever had to do is:

_____

11. My favorite sport to play is:

_____

12. My favorite sport to watch is:

_____

13. If I could travel in time, I would visit:

_____

14. When I have free time, I love to:

_____

15. If I was president for a month, I would:

_____

16. The thing I am best at is:

_____

17. My favorite ice cream flavor is:

_____

18. The coolest place I have ever been is:

_____

19. If I could pick any superpower, I'd pick:

_____

20. Someday, I want to invent:

_____

21. If I were in a band, I would play:

_____

22. When I am feeling sad, what helps me start to feel better is:

_____

23. If I had 10 million dollars, I would:

_____

24. My favorite song is:

_____

25. I do / do not (*circle one*) like having pets because:

_____

26. I make other people laugh when I:

_____

27. One thing that makes me really proud of myself is:

_____

28. A positive change I made about myself was:

_____

29. The thing that scares me the most is:

_____

30. The best thing about being me is:

_____

KEY POINT

Did you notice that none of the questions on the list are about race, politics, religion, or the amount of money your family has? That's because these things are not important when it comes to making friends. *Never let the differences between you and someone else keep you from becoming friends*. Remember that it's easy to become friends with people who live very differently when you have the same interests, hobbies, or skills.

- Use the **30 Questions for Kids** with a friend.
  - Ask your friend each question, then compare your answers.
  - This is a fun way to get to know someone. Share laughs as you talk about your answers!
- Consider using the **30 Questions** with a whole group of kids.
  - Try to guess who wrote which answer.
  - You'll learn new things about people you thought you knew well. Besides, it's a lot of fun trying to figure out who said what!

Key 2: Reach Out to People You Trust

CHECKPOINT

1. **Next to each statement, write down if it is a TATTLING rule or a TELLING rule:**

   a. Someone is hurt and needs help:

   _____

   b. The person did it by accident and is sorry:

   _____

   c. This is a "So What?" problem:

   _____

   d. There is a *P*attern to what is going on:

   _____

   e. Your goal is to keep someone safe:

   _____

2. **Circle the best answer**:

   When writing a Safety Plan, you should think about connecting with adults who:

   a. talk more than they listen

   b. will take you seriously

   c. live too far away to help

3. **Match the definition with the word or phrase it describes**:

   _____ Anonymous   **a.** Get to know all kinds of different kids

   _____ Confidential   **b.** You don't have to give your name

   _____ Cast a wide net   **c.** A trustworthy adult doesn't share your name

4. **Write True or False next to each statement**:

   a. _____ You can only make friends with kids who belong to the same race, share the same religion, and have an equal amount of money.

   b. _____ Sharing interests, hobbies, and skills can help you connect with kids who help you feel great.

Key 2: Reach Out to People You Trust

 CHECKPOINT

A N S W E R   K E Y

1. **Next to each statement, write down if it is a TATTLING rule or a TELLING rule:**

   a. Someone is hurt and needs help:

   Telling

   b. The person did it by accident and is sorry:

   Tatttling

   c. This is a "So What?" problem:

   Tattling

   d. There is a **P**attern to what is going on:

   Telling

   e. Your goal is to keep someone safe:

   Telling

2. **Circle the best answer**:

When writing a **Safety Plan**, you should think about connecting with adults who:

a. talk more than they listen

(b.) will take you seriously

c. live too far away to help

3. **Match the definition with the word or phrase it describes:**

_____ Anonymous   **a.** Get to know all kinds of different kids

_____ Confidential   **b.** You don't have to give your name

_____ Cast a wide net   **c.** A trustworthy adult doesn't share your name

4. **Write True or False next to each statement**:

a. _False_ You can only make friends with kids who belong to the same race, share the same religion, and have an equal amount of money.

b. _True_ Sharing interests, hobbies, and skills can help you connect with kids who help you feel great.

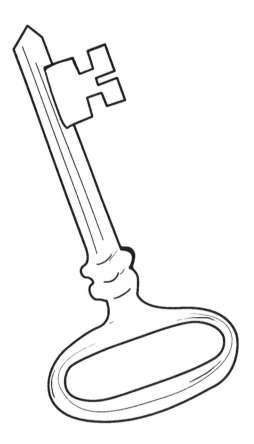

KEY 2: *I know how to connect with people I trust!*

3

STOP BULLYING
WHENEVER YOU SEE IT

ACTIVITY 10: WORDS MATTER!

WORDS MATTER. The words you use and your tone of voice affect how other people feel. In this Activity, you will learn to choose words that build strong friendships.

You will need 2 items for this Activity. These items will help you remember how certain words and phrases make people feel. Before moving on, gather:

- ✓ A cotton ball
- ✓ A piece of sandpaper

THINK ABOUT IT

Have you ever heard this old rhyme?

> *Sticks and stones*
> *may break my bones,*
> *but words*
> *will never hurt me.*

If you have, *try to forget you ever heard it!* (If you haven't, try to forget I ever mentioned it!) Anyone who has ever been called a cruel name or been yelled at by a friend knows that words really can cause pain! To really get a *feel* for what I'm talking about, try this experiment:

EXPERIMENT

Step 1: Take the cotton ball in your hand. Move it between your fingers. Notice how it feels on your skin.

Step 2: In the space below, (circle) the words that describe how the cotton feels:

rough	soft	fuzzy	bumpy
smooth	gentle	hard	scraping
ouch	nice	painful	good

Step 3: Now, rub your fingers back and forth across the piece of sandpaper. Notice how different it feels from the cotton ball.

Step 4: In the space below, draw a box around the words that describe how the sandpaper feels:

rough	soft	fuzzy	bumpy
smooth	gentle	hard	scraping
ouch	nice	painful	good

Cotton & Sandpaper

If you think about it, words can be a lot like cotton and sandpaper. Some words make us feel good and fuzzy like cotton, while other words are rough and cause pain, like sandpaper. Can you think of real-life examples of cotton and sandpaper words?

"Cotton words" are things like compliments, good manners, and giving encouragement to others.

IN THE SPACE BELOW, WRITE DOWN SOME EXAMPLES OF COTTON WORDS THAT COME TO YOUR MIND.

EXAMPLE:

Good job!

_____   _____

_____   _____

How do you feel when someone speaks to you with cotton words?

_____

"Sandpaper words" are used to put down, tease, and even tattle on others.

In the space below, write down examples of sandpaper words that you have heard used to hurt kids.

EXAMPLE:

Stupid!

_____   _____

_____   _____

How do you feel when someone speaks to you with sandpaper words?

_____

It's easy to understand why most people like to spend time with "cotton talkers." It's also clear why kids avoid making friends with "sandpaper mouths." Next, you'll practice choosing between cotton and sandpaper words.

Cotton & Sandpaper Words:

Directions:

Read each statement below. Circle "Cotton" if the statement represents warm, kind words. Circle "Sandpaper" if the statement is an example of rough or bullying language.

1.	Please stop calling me names.	Cotton	Sandpaper
2.	You're calling me names! You're mean.	Cotton	Sandpaper
3.	I'm sorry I bumped into you. It was an accident.	Cotton	Sandpaper
4.	It's so embarrassing when you tell people my secrets. Will you please keep them to yourself?	Cotton	Sandpaper
5.	If you don't stop, I'm going to take your Legos!	Cotton	Sandpaper
6.	You butted in line. I'm telling on you!	Cotton	Sandpaper
7.	I asked you to stop touching me, but you're not listening. If you do it again, I am going to ask the teacher for help.	Cotton	Sandpaper
8.	Can I please play with you guys?	Cotton	Sandpaper
9.	I can't see! Get out of my way!	Cotton	Sandpaper
10.	Can you please sit down so I can see?	Cotton	Sandpaper
11.	Please stop laughing at me.	Cotton	Sandpaper
12.	I'm not your friend anymore!	Cotton	Sandpaper
13.	You can't play with us!	Cotton	Sandpaper
14.	You cheated! I hate you.	Cotton	Sandpaper
15.	Give me that back! It's mine!	Cotton	Sandpaper

Do you know the difference between cotton and sandpaper words? An Answer Key is provided at the end of this Activity for you to check your responses.

KEY POINT

It's common in elementary and middle schools for kids to become known for certain talents and skills. Some kids are known for being great artists or star athletes. Others play an instrument, shine on stage, or get straight A's.

Make it your goal to be known for being kind.

Choose cotton words whenever you can. Avoid sandpaper words at all times. Make friends with other kids who do the same. These are the friends that help you feel good about yourself.

USE MARKERS, COLORED PENCILS OR CRAYONS TO DECORATE YOUR OWN KINDESS RIBBON

This Activity has been adapted for use in this workbook from "Cotton vs. sandpaper words," https://theschoolcounselorkind.wordpress.com/2013/12/26/cotton-vs-sandpaper-words/. Used by permission of the author.

Cotton and Sandpaper Words

A N S W E R   K E Y

1.	Please stop calling me names.	(Cotton)	Sandpaper
2.	You're calling me names! You're mean.	Cotton	(Sandpaper)
3.	I'm sorry I bumped into you. It was an accident.	(Cotton)	Sandpaper
4.	It's so embarrassing when you tell people my secrets. Will you please keep them to yourself?	(Cotton)	Sandpaper
5.	If you don't stop, I'm going to take your Legos!	Cotton	(Sandpaper)
6.	You butted in line. I'm telling on you!	Cotton	(Sandpaper)
7.	I asked you to stop touching me, but you're not listening. If you do it again, I am going to ask the teacher for help.	(Cotton)	Sandpaper
8.	Can I please play with you guys?	(Cotton)	Sandpaper
9.	I can't see! Get out of my way!	Cotton	(Sandpaper)
10.	Can you please sit down so I can see?	(Cotton)	Sandpaper
11.	Please stop laughing at me.	(Cotton)	Sandpaper
12.	I'm not your friend anymore!	Cotton	(Sandpaper)
13.	You can't play with us!	Cotton	(Sandpaper)
14.	You cheated! I hate you.	Cotton	(Sandpaper)
15.	Give me that back! It's mine!	Cotton	(Sandpaper)

ACTIVITY 11: QUIZ TIME: WHAT'S MY REPLY?

IN ACTIVITY 10, you learned that *words matter* when it comes to making friends. In this Activity, you'll learn even more about the style of words that is best for stopping bullying.

THINK ABOUT IT

When it comes to getting dressed each day, we all have our own style. Some kids like to wear sporty clothing. Others prefer to dress up. For many, extras rule—cool hats, glittery headbands, funny T-shirts, and stylish shoes are a must.

The truth is, style isn't just about clothing. You express your style each day by the way you reply to others. When it comes to standing up for yourself in a bullying situation, your "Reply Style" can decide how quickly the bullying ends.

Read each real-life situation from the *What's My Reply?* quiz below. Then, choose the reply you think would be best for stopping bullying. At the end of the quiz, we'll review your answers and talk about the best style for stopping bullying.

What's My Reply?

1. You are working on a computer at school when a classmate comes over and says, "It's my turn!" He puts his hand on the back of your chair and starts to slide it out from the desk. You can no longer reach the keyboard. You:

A. Shove him away and shout, "If you touch my chair again, I'll hit you!"

B. Get up right away and give him the computer, even though you're not done with your work.

C. Look him in the eye and say, "Please don't push my chair. You can have the computer as soon as I save my work."

2. On the bus home from school, a kid throws your book bag out of the back seat, saying that it's reserved for "5th-graders only." You tell her:

A. "The 5th-graders are the biggest losers in the whole school!"

B. "Okay, sorry."

C. "I didn't know this seat was reserved. Next time, please tell me instead of throwing my stuff."

3. Kayla used to be your best friend. Lately, though, she's been hanging around with Abby. She barely talks to you anymore. This morning, she is extra nice to you and then says, "Can I copy your math homework? I forgot to do it last night!" You reply:

A. "Yeah, right. Now you want to be my friend again? Go ask Abby, since you like her so much more than you like me!"

B. "Sure, Kayla."

C. "I would, but I don't want to get in trouble. I can explain it to you if you need help."

4. Out of the blue, Jonah texts you this message: "No one likes you. Why do you even come to school? You should just be homeschooled!" You:

A. Text a note to everyone in your class that says, "Jonah is the biggest loser in school. He'll never have a girlfriend because he is so ugly."

B. Start to cry, then delete the message before your mom or dad see it.

C. Take a screen shot of the text and show it to your teacher at school. Then block Jonah from texting you anymore.

5. You and Nolan are playing video games at your house after school. Nolan gets upset because you win 3 games in a row. He throws down his controller and says, "It's not fair! You're cheating!" You reply:

A. "Don't be such a whiny baby, Nolan. I can't help it if you stink at video games."

B. "It's my fault, Nolan. I shouldn't have played so hard. We can say that you won that round."

C. "I can tell you're not having fun anymore. Let's play something else. Just be careful of my controller—I don't want you to break my things."

What's My Reply? Quiz Choices:

Look back on the answers you chose for each of the 5 situations above:

In each of the situations, the "A" response shows MEAN behavior. Just like the Tiger responses from Activity 5, *Mean* responses may be a natural instinct, but they are also a sure way to make a conflict worse. Plus, have you ever noticed that adults usually notice the person who reacted with Mean behavior before they realize that someone else started it? Be smart in your replies to others. Never confuse feeling better for a moment with solving a problem once and for all!

In each of the situations, the "B" response shows MEEK behavior.

"*Meek*" rhymes with "weak." Sadly, people who use Meek words—such as saying sorry when it isn't their fault or letting others hurt them—are thought of as weak by kids who bully. This weakness gives bullies a green light to keep hurting their victims over and over again.

Some people choose Meek replies because they are trying to be nice. Others choose Meekness because they want to avoid a fight. While these are both good goals, remember that *being known for being kind* is not the same as allowing other people to hurt you. Standing up for yourself with the "Mean-It" behaviors described next is always the best way to stop bullying.

In each of the situations, the "C" response shows MEAN-IT behavior.

Mean-It replies let the other person know that you mean what you say and say what you mean. You speak in a way that is honest but still polite and kind. You do not hurt others with your Mean-It voice, and you do not allow them to continue to hurt you.

You can show someone that you really *Mean It* when you:

- Look the person straight in the eye
- Speak in a strong, even voice
- Use clear words to tell the person what you do or do not want to have happen.

KEY POINT

Remember: Kids who bully are not looking for a fair fight! Their goal is to have **P**ower over someone else. They are looking for kids who either overreact with *Mean* behavior or underreact with *Meekness*. **When you show that you *Mean* It, you pick the perfect reply for stopping bullying before it can ever really get started.**

WRITE ABOUT IT

In the space below, write your own What's My Reply? quiz question.

- First, describe a situation from your real life where someone used bullying behavior.
- Then, write down 3 choices—one *Mean*, one *Meek*, and one *Mean-It*—for how a person could reply.
- Challenge a family member or friend to take your quiz.
- Talk to them about their Reply Style. If they chose a *Mean* or *Meek* answer, help them think about how they could make a better choice to bring an end to the bullying.

QUIZ QUESTION:

_____

_____

_____

_____

REPLY CHOICES:

a. _____

b. _____

c. _____

ACTIVITY 12: MEAN, MEEK, OR MEAN-IT

IN THE LAST ACTIVITY, you learned the difference between *Mean, Meek,* and *Mean-It* words to reply to bullying. Kids who use *Mean-It* words are best at stopping bad situations from becoming worse. In this Activity, you will learn how important your tone of voice is in supporting your words.

THINK ABOUT IT

Just as you can lower your voice to whisper in a library and raise your voice to cheer for your favorite team, you can control the tone of your voice to respond well to bullying. In this Activity, you will learn to use your voice as a tool for stopping bullying.

Directions:

Read each statement on page 72 aloud 3 times using these rules:

1. The first time, use a *Mean* voice that expresses anger.
2. The second time, use a *Meek* voice that expresses fear or sadness.
3. The third time, use a strong, confident *Mean-It* voice that shows that you mean what you say and say what you mean.

To make this activity even more eye-opening, try these extra steps:

- Use a tablet or smartphone to record yourself saying each statement aloud in the 3 different voices. Play back the recording to hear how each Reply Style sounds.
- Read the statements aloud to a parent, brother, sister, or trusted friend. Ask them to tell you how your tone of voice supports your words.

STATEMENTS

1. Please turn down the volume on the TV.

2. I didn't say you were upset.

3. Can you pass the pasta?

4. What did you say?

5. Excuse me.

6. Stop it.

7. What were you thinking when you did that?

8. I need your help.

9. I'd like you to stop saying that.

10. That's not funny.

MORE TO THINK ABOUT

1. How did the meaning of each statement change depending on the tone of voice you used? (Match the correct responses.)

A Mean voice made me seem: powerful and confident

A Meek voice made me seem: angry and unkind

A Mean-It voice made me seem: weak and scared

2. How do you think someone would respond to you if you said something in a *Mean* tone of voice? (Circle all that apply.)

    a. The person might want to fight me.

    b. The person might think I'm really nice.

    c. The person might be scared and avoid me.

    d. The person might tell a teacher on me.

3. How could using a *Meek* voice make a situation worse? (Circle all that apply.)

    a. It could make the person think I am weak and easy to control.

    b. It could make the person think I don't know how to stand up for myself.

    c. It could make me look strong and respected.

    d. It could make me look as if I am ready for a fight.

4. In your own words, explain why a *Mean-It* voice is best for stopping bullying.

_____

_____

An Answer Key for these questions is provided on the next page.

MORE TO THINK ABOUT

A N S W E R   K E Y

1. How did the meaning of each statement change depending on the tone of voice you used? (Match the correct responses.)

A Mean voice made me seem: ——————————— powerful and confident

A Meek voice made me seem: ——————————— angry and unkind

A Mean-It voice made me seem: ——————————— weak and scared

2. How do you think someone would respond to you if you said something in a *Mean* tone of voice? (Circle all that apply.)

(a.) The person might want to fight me.

b. The person might think I'm really nice.

(c.) The person might be scared and avoid me.

(d.) The person might tell a teacher on me.

3. How could using a *Meek* voice make a situation worse? (Circle all that apply.)

(a.) It could make the person think I am weak and easy to control.

(b.) It could make the person think I don't know how to stand up for myself.

c. It could make me look strong and respected.

d. It could make me look as if I am ready for a fight.

4. In your own words, explain why a *Mean-It* voice is best for stopping bullying.

A Mean-It voice shows that you mean what you say and say what you mean. You do not hurt other people and do not allow them to hurt you.

There are many possible correct responses. If you wrote something like the sentences above, you are on the right track!

ACTIVITY 13: WHAT TO SAY IN A BULLYING SITUATION

HAVE YOU EVER BEEN IN A SITUATION where someone says or does something cruel to you and you freeze up? You wish you could think of something clever to say to stand up for yourself. You search your brain for a funny joke that would make everyone laugh. Instead, all you can come up with is a blank stare. Or maybe words do come to your mouth, but they end up being *Mean* or *Meek* responses that make things worse. In this Activity, you'll learn specific *Mean-It* phrases—suggested by kids just like you—so that when bullying occurs, you are ready to respond well.

THINK ABOUT IT

In this Activity Book, you have learned that you always have *choices* when it comes to how to respond to conflict and bullying. The words you use and the tone of voice you choose to respond to the cruelty of others can control how often (and how badly) you are bullied. Because you have the power to choose a helpful response, you need never let a hurtful person put you in a powerless position. That's great news!

Here's another little secret: Kids who are good at acting as if other kids' put-downs or cruel behavior don't even bother them are best at stopping bullying in its tracks.

So, what do smart kids say to show others that they think the bullying is lame? There are lots of words to choose from. You'll learn many of them in the activity below. **What they all**

have in common is that they all make bullying BORING. Yes, that's right. Kids who bully feel **P**owerful when they can get a big reaction out of people (like a *Mean* comeback or a *Meek* reply.) When you act like you don't care what the bully said, you make bullying boring for them. Better yet, you take away the bully's power over you. This make it far less likely that you'll be bullied again.

Now that you know this little secret, spread the word! Seriously, tell everyone you know this simple choice for responding. It's so easy—and works so well!

Mixed-Up Mean-It Comebacks

Directions:

Banish the "brain freeze" of being caught off guard by bullying! Never be at a loss for words again! Unscramble each of the phrases below to reveal a helpful comeback to bullying.

1. htW'as uory ontpi? _____

2. oNt oolc. _____

3. rateevhW _____

4. h'Ttas os otn nynuf. _____

5. fl oyu ays os. _____

6. hTat dssnou ielk a mourr ot em. _____

7. I eilk het ywa I ookl. _____

8. yyAawn. _____

9. kKcno ti fof. _____

10. lelT em nweh ouy etg ot het nyufn tarp. _____

An Answer Key is provided at the end of this Activity.

Now you know 10 new phrases for responding to bullying. Remember to say them in a *Mean-It* tone of voice. Look the person in the eye as you are speaking. These are simple but powerful actions. They tell others that you are strong. They let people knowing that continuing to tease or bully you won't be any fun at all.

THE BEST COMEBACKS sound natural when you say them aloud. Are there any phrases from the Activity that do not seem like they would come out of your mouth? If so, that's okay! We all have our own way of speaking. If any of the phrases on the list sound strange to you, they won't sound real when you say them. In the space below, write down 3 to 4 original *Mean-It* comebacks that you will feel comfortable using in a bullying situation:

_____   _____

_____   _____

To get these comebacks to work even better, practice saying them in front of a mirror. Use a natural, *Mean-It* tone of voice. Better still, grab a brother. sister, friend, or parent. Practice saying these words out loud to them. Ask them what you could do to say them even better. Using the advice they give you will help you reply well in a real-life bullying situation.

Mixed-Up Mean-It Comebacks

A N S W E R   K E Y

1. What's your point?

2. Not cool.

3. Whatever.

4. That's so not funny.

5. If you say so.

6. That sounds like a rumor to me.

7. I like the way I look.

8. Anyway.

9. Knock it off.

10. Tell me when you get to the funny part.

Key 3: Stop Bullying When You See It

CHECKPOINT

1. Decide whether each phrase below is a Cotton way to talk or a Sandpaper way to talk. Write each phrase in the correct column:

Great job!	Way to go, loser!	Get out of my way!
May I please have one?	Shut up!	Would you like to play?
Give it to me now!	I'll make space for you here.	Are you okay?

Cotton Words:

_____

_____

_____

_____

_____

Sandpaper words:

_____

_____

_____

_____

_____

2. Sandpaper words are usually spoken in a _____.
(Circle 1 answer.)

  a. *Mean* voice

  b. *Meek* voice

  c. *Mean-It* voice

3. One big problem with *Mean* and *Meek* responses is that they usually just make a situation _____. (Circle 1 answer.)

    a. better

    b. worse

    c. stay the same

4. When using a *Mean-It* response, it is best to also _____. (Circle all that apply.)

    a. avoid eye contact

    b. look the person in the eye

    c. use a strong, even voice

    d. yell as loudly as you can

5. Kids who are good at acting as if other people's put-downs don't bother them are the _____ at stopping bullying in its tracks. (Circle 1 answer.)

    a. best

    b. worst

    c. lamest

USE THIS FREE SPACE TO TRACE YOUR HANDPRINT. ON EACH FINGER, WRITE A *MEAN-IT* PRASE YOU CAN USE TO RESPOND TO BULLYING.

Key 3: Stop Bullying Whenever You See It

☑ CHECKPOINT

A N S W E R   K E Y

1. Decide whether each phrase below is a Cotton way to talk or a Sandpaper way to talk. Write each phrase in the correct column:

Great job!	Way to go, loser!	Get out of my way!
May I please have one?	Shut up!	Would you like to play?
Give it to me now!	I'll make space for you here.	Are you okay?

Cotton Words:

Great job!

May I please have one?

Would you like to play?

I'll make space for you here.

Are you okay?

Sandpaper words:

Way to go, loser!

Get out of my way!

Shut up!

Give it to me now!

_____

2. Sandpaper words are usually spoken in a _____.
(Circle 1 answer.)

(a.) Mean voice
b. Meek voice
c. Mean-It voice

3. One big problem with *Mean* and *Meek* responses is that they usually just make a situation _____. (Circle 1 answer.)

    a. better

    (**b.**) worse

    c. stay the same

4. When using a *Mean-It* response, it is best to also _____. (Circle all that apply.)

    a. avoid eye contact

    (**b.**) look the person in the eye

    (**c.**) use a strong, even voice

    d. yell as loudly as you can

5. Kids who are good at acting as if other people's put-downs don't bother them are the _____ at stopping bullying in its tracks. (Circle 1 answer.)

    (**a.**) best

    b. worst

    c. lamest

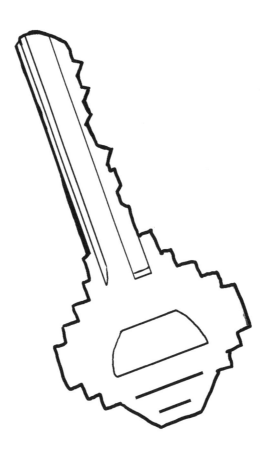

KEY 3: *I know how to stop bullying whenever I see it!*

BE CYBERBULLYING FREE

ACTIVITY 14: WHAT'S YOUR FAVORITE APP?

WHAT IS YOUR FIRST MEMORY of using a computer, tablet, or smartphone? Since you are growing up in the 21st century, your childhood is likely filled with gadgets—for information, for shopping, for texting, for passing time while standing in line, and best of all, for fun! There are so many great uses for technology. This Activity will help you think about all the things you enjoy about growing up in a "plugged-in" world.

THINK ABOUT IT

Do the adults in your life enjoy using technology as much as you do? Today, people of most ages own gadgets like smartphones, laptops, tablets, and gaming devices. Many of us use them several times each day—if not all day! And yet you may know adults who seem concerned about your use of gadgets. Why do you think the very adults who love their own technology get so concerned about your tech use?

The truth is, as handy and fun as technology is, it also creates real dangers for young people. Adults are right to have concerns, especially about safety, friendships, and bullying. There are ways you can assure adults that you are using your gadgets in safe, fun, respectful ways. One of the best ways is to show them that you understand their worries. Make it clear that you have thought through what is good and bad about your devices. The questions in this Activity are designed to help you do that.

GADGETS, GAMES, & ME

Directions:

Read each question below. Think carefully about your answer. In the space provided, write down your response.

Consider sharing your thoughts and ideas with a parent, relative, teacher, or other caring adult who can be there for you if you ever need help or advice.

1. What is your favorite app, website, or video game?

_____

_____

2. What do you like best about it?

_____

_____

3. About how often do you visit this app/site/game? (Circle the best answer.)

About once a month	About once a week	About once a day
A few times each month	A few times each week	A few times each day

4. Do you interact with your friends on this app/site/game? (Check one.)

☐ Yes, I like to play this game/app with others.

☐ No, this is an app/site/game I usually use alone.

5. Has using this app/site/game helped you become closer with certain friends? Has it hurt any of your relationships? Explain.

_____

_____

6. How is this app/site/game used to cyberbully? (Check all that apply.)

What's up LOSER??

☐ It isn't.

☐ People can post cruel comments.

☐ People can post embarrassing photos.

☐ People can post anonymously.

☐ People can forward messages or photos without the sender's permission.

☐ People can be kicked out of the chat/game on purpose.

☐ Other: _____

7. Have you ever seen people be cruel to each other on this app/site/game? What do you do if this happens?

_____

_____

8. Does this app/site/game ever add to your FOMO (fear of missing out?). If so, how? How do you handle it?

_____

_____

---

9. If you could create your own app, social media site, or video game, what would it be like? In the lined area below, give it a name. Describe it in your own words. Then, use the open space to sketch your creation's home screen.

NAME:

_____

DESCRIPTION:

_____

_____

_____

HOME SCREEN SKETCH

ACTIVITY 15: 5 "BESTS" OF TECHNOLOGY

- WHAT IS YOUR FAVORITE MOVIE?

- IF YOU COULD GO ANYWHERE IN THE WORLD FOR A DAY, WHERE WOULD YOU GO?

- WHICH ICE CREAM FLAVOR IS THE VERY BEST?

You have many "favorites" and "bests" in your life. This Activity will help you think through the 5 best things about the technology you use.

THINK ABOUT IT

Summer vacation is awesome—but sometimes it does get too hot. Dessert is the best part of any meal—except when you're already too full. There are good sides and bad sides to everything in life. This is also true of technology. In this activity, you'll focus on the best things about smartphones, social media, the Internet, and gaming. You'll also learn how to turn negatives (such as cyberbullying) into positives.

5 "Bests" of Today's Technology

A. Make a list of at least 5 ways that technology helps you have fun and connect with others:

1.
2.
3.
4.
5.

B. Now, using the table on page 92, list 5 ways that technology can be used to hurt someone. Write your answer on the left side of the table, under "Hurtful Uses of Technology."

C. Next, for each negative item listed on the left, use the line on the right side of the table to write at least 1 positive thing you could do to make the bad situation better. An example is provided.

HURTFUL USES OF TECHNOLOGY	WAYS TO FIX THE PROBLEM
1. *Example:* Posting an embarrassing photo of someone	1. *Example:* • Take a screen shot and show it to a helpful adult • Delete the photo from my device • Tell the sender to stop • If it's posted on social media, use the app's anonymous reporting system
2.	2.
3.	3.
4.	4.
5.	5.

KEY POINT

Anytime you turn a negative into a positive in your life, you show that you are responsible and respectful. It's normal for adults who care about you to worry about the dangers of cyberbullying. These adults are showing that they care for you when they limit your use of gadgets. Every time you turn what could be a problem into a smart solution, you earn an adult's trust. You also show them you are mature enough to enjoy all the great things technology offers.

ACTIVITY 16: RULES OF NETIQUETTE

WHAT HAPPENS IN CYBERSPACE stays in cyberspace—forever! Why does this matter? Because someday you will apply to college, interview for your dream job, and even meet your future in-laws. For all of these occasions (and more!), you will want people to think highly of you. While one of the great parts about being young is the freedom to live in the moment, you can avoid making short-sighted decisions now that will damage your reputation in the future.

THINK ABOUT IT

In this section, you will find 10 guidelines for using technology—cell phones, texting, apps, social media, computers, tablets, gaming devices, and so on—in ways that are fun for you, safe for your future, and respectful of others.

Put a bookmark in this page of your Activity Book or tear out the Rules of Netiquette and post them somewhere where you can read and review them often.

Rules of Netiquette

RULE 1: Choose Your Words Carefully

If you wouldn't say something to a person's face, don't text it or post it online. Technology makes it too easy to say things that are unkind. Also, the person reading your message can't see the look on your face or hear the tone of your voice. Trying to be sarcastic or funny doesn't always come across online. *Type carefully as well.* Don't use ALL CAPS, since they make it look as if you are angry or YELLING. #dontsaydontsend

RULE 2: The Internet Is Not a Weapon

Don't gossip about other people through texts or online. It's not okay to talk about people behind their backs. Also, social media sites should not be used to leave people out or to "de-friend" a person after a fight.

RULE 3: Who Is This Message For?

Though you may think you are sending a private message or photo to one friend, keep in mind . that it can be cut, pasted, and forwarded to an endless number of people. Never post a photo or message that you wouldn't want "everyone" to be able to view.

Be thoughtful about the photos and videos that you allow your friends to take of you. Sometimes, these photos start off as fun, but they can be used in embarrassing ways later on. Always have all of your clothes on in pictures and videos. Seriously.

RULE 4: What You Post Is Permanent

Once you share something online, you lose control of where it goes, who can forward it, who will see it, and how it can be used. You might believe right now that you can trust your best friend with secrets, but you should not send personal information online. You can't imagine it now, but someday, that information could be twisted and used against you.

Commit to a kindness-only policy for your posts. Do not ever use technology to say ugly or mean things about anyone or to anyone. Stop and ask yourself, "What would Mom think if she read this?" Post accordingly.

RULE 5: Take It Slow

The online world can be very fast paced. You may be tempted to say whatever comes to your mind in a given moment. Don't do it! Slow down and think before you post. Wait until you have had a chance to think things through. Cool your head before you post a message that can't be taken back.

RULE 6: Report It

Most social media websites have easy, anonymous reporting systems. Anytime you learn that cyberbullying is taking place, report it right away. The site will take down the content, and you can feel good knowing that you took action to help yourself or another victim of cyberbullying. For most social media sites, the general reporting address is: abuse@websitename.com

RULE 7: Unplug Every Once in a While

A first step in stopping cyberbullying is logging off from an account temporarily. You can instantly end a digital conversation and should plan to do so the minute you recognize that cruelty has begun. In cases where unkindness is repeated, block the person altogether.

RULE 8: Don't Talk to Strangers

Remember that message your parents gave you when you were little? It still applies today and is very important to remember when you are online. Strangers hide in cyberspace and have clever ways of learning about you. Never share private information online, including your full name, home address, personal photos, school name, or phone number.

The same is true for "followers" on social media sites. There is a very, very, VERY big difference between real friends and online followers. Remember that quality of friendships is much more important than quantity. Plan to spend most of your time and energy on your real-life friendships rather than on anonymous cyber-followers.

RULE 9: Set Strong Passwords

Set strong passwords on all of your accounts. Make sure that the only person who is speaking for you is YOU.

RULE 10: It's (NOT!) Nice to Share

For most of your life, you've been told that it's nice to share with others. When it comes to your passwords, though, just DON'T do it! Your accounts are *your* accounts. Don't let any friend—even a best friend—post or text from your account. Ever.

The exception to this rule is your parents. DO share your passwords with them. Don't think of it as invading your privacy. Know that this is the best way for your parents to keep you safe from harm.

WRITE ABOUT IT

*These 10 basic Rules are just a start. In the space below, add your own rules
for using technology safely and respectfully.*

More Rules of Netiquette

_____

_____

_____

_____

_____

_____

_____

_____

_____

_____

_____

_____

_____

_____

_____

_____

_____

_____

ACTIVITY 17: TO SEND OR NOT TO SEND?

DO YOU HAVE YOUR OWN SMARTPHONE? Now you do—at least on paper! In this Activity, you'll get to design a case for your phone. Be creative, use color, and have fun creating a case that is uniquely YOU! Then, you'll have the opportunity to think through whether or not certain messages typed on your new phone should be sent—or deleted immediately!

THINK ABOUT IT

To Send or Not to Send? is a follow-up to Activity 16, in which you learned the Rules of Netiquette. Now, you'll put the *Rules* to work!

Directions:

- First, use the space on the next page to design your own smartphone case and home screen.
- Then, read real-life texts, emails, and posts from other people's phones. Decide whether or not they should be sent.

's Smartphone

MY HOME SCREEN

MY SMARTPHONE CASE

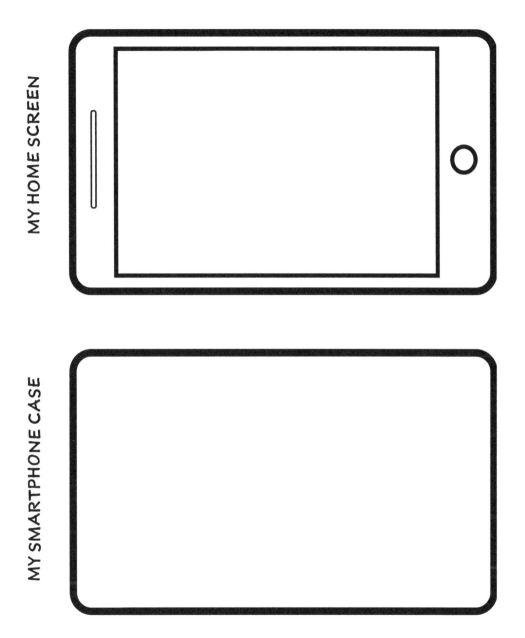

To Send or Not to Send?

Directions:

Beneath each smartphone screen, circle the word **SEND** if you think the message follows the Rules of Netiquette. Circle **DELETE** if you think the message would hurt a friendship or someone's feelings.

An Answer Key is provided at the end of this activity.

PHONE 1

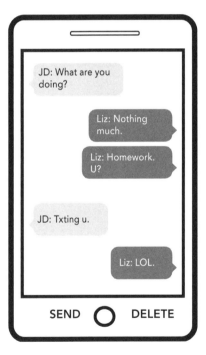

PHONE 2

PHONE 3

@LucyLC I deleted u and unfollowed u. No one likes u and u r going 2 b alone ur whole life.

SEND ◯ DELETE

PHONE 4

Hey—
Do you want to go to the movies on Friday, then sleepover? Emily and Aimee are coming too. Lmk.

SEND ◯ DELETE

PHONE 5

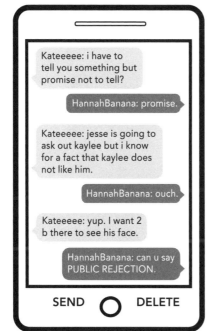

Kateeeee: i have to tell you something but promise not to tell?

HannahBanana: promise.

Kateeeee: jesse is going to ask out kaylee but i know for a fact that kaylee does not like him.

HannahBanana: ouch.

Kateeeee: yup. I want 2 b there to see his face.

HannahBanana: can u say PUBLIC REJECTION.

SEND ◯ DELETE

PHONE 6

Mayamaya: Still coming over to hang out?

LMZ3: omg. totally forgot! made other plans.

Mayamaya: Seriously?

LMZ3: so sorry! I'll totally make it up to you!

Mayamaya: No way. You ruined my whole night. I could have gone to Stacy's house but I told her I was hanging out with you. I hate you.

SEND ◯ DELETE

To Send or Not to Send?

ANSWER KEY

Phone 1: SEND

This is a fun text between friends. It can be sent with no worries.

Phone 2: DELETE

Social media should never be used to hurt someone or make them feel excluded on purpose. This post seems to have no purpose other than to make the other person feel left out. It should be deleted.

Phone 3: DELETE

The Internet is not a weapon. Never send a message with hateful, cruel words—even if you are really, really mad at someone. Delete a post like this before the way you're feeling now turns into permanent cruelty.

Phone 4: SEND

Email is a great way to send brief messages and make plans with friends. This email can be sent!

Phone 5: DELETE

Don't use your phone to gossip, spread rumors, or take joy in someone else's pain. These texts just show how low Kateeeee and HannahBanana can go. They should be deleted before ever being sent.

Phone 6: DELETE

Mayamaya may have a right to be angry, but she does not have a right to text (or speak!) to LMZ3 that way. She should delete this text before her friendship is ruined for good.

ACTIVITY 18: WHEN YOUR MESSAGE GETS MIXED UP ONLINE

HAVE YOU EVER BEEN INSULTED BY A TEXT, post, message, or email from a friend? Maybe you couldn't get over how rude or thoughtless the person was. Did you run into the person later and hear them speak the same words out loud, then realize they had just been trying to be funny?

In this Activity, you'll see how talking online is different from talking face-to-face. You'll learn new ways to check on the meaning of online messages you're not sure about.

THINK ABOUT IT

In Activity 11, you learned about *Mean*, *Meek*, and *Mean-It* responses. Then, in Activity 12, you learned about how tone of voice changes the meaning of your messages. But what happens when you say something in a text or online and there is no tone of voice to go with it? If there are no *Mean*, *Meek*, and *Mean-It* tones online, how can you know what a person is truly saying to you—and how to best respond?

Directions:

For this activity, you will need red, yellow, and green pencils or crayons.

PART 1: READ THE SITUATION BELOW.

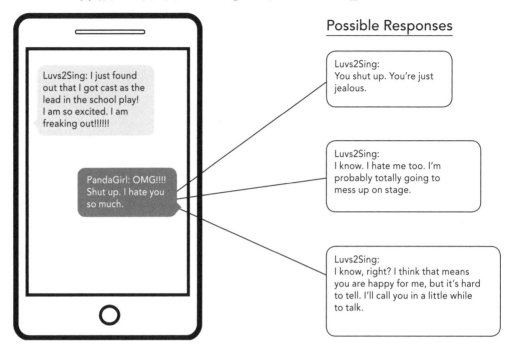

Possible Responses

Luvs2Sing: I just found out that I got cast as the lead in the school play! I am so excited. I am freaking out!!!!!!

PandaGirl: OMG!!!! Shut up. I hate you so much.

Luvs2Sing:
You shut up. You're just jealous.

Luvs2Sing:
I know. I hate me too. I'm probably totally going to mess up on stage.

Luvs2Sing:
I know, right? I think that means you are happy for me, but it's hard to tell. I'll call you in a little while to talk.

PART 2: USING YOUR COLORED PENCILS OR CRAYONS, SHADE EACH RESPONSE ABOVE AS FOLLOWS:

- The first possible response is **Mean**. It would insult PandaGirl and make the situation worse. Color it RED.

- The second possible response is **Meek**. Luvs2Sing takes PandaGirl's text literally and responds by downplaying her good news. Color it YELLOW.

- The third possible response is a **Mean-It** one. This text is honest and direct without being mean or meek. Talking to someone in person is the best way to clear up any confusing online messages. Color it GREEN.

PART 3: IN THE SPACE BELOW, WRITE IN YOUR OWN POSSIBLE MEAN, MEEK, AND MEAN-IT RESPONSES TO THE TEXT CONVERSATION.

- Color the **Mean** response red, the **Meek** response yellow, and the **Mean-It** response green.
- Whenever you respond to an unclear text or online post, make sure that the only response you give a GREEN light to is a *Mean-It* one. #thinkbeforeyoupost

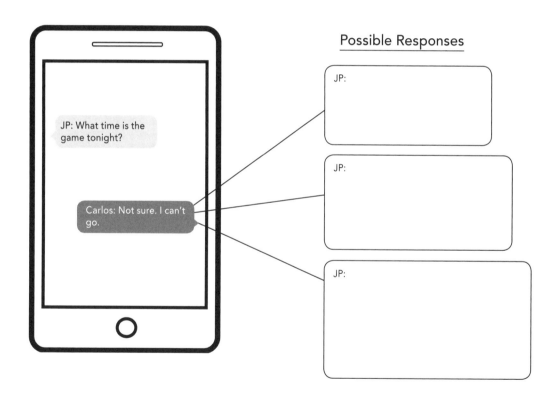

Possible Responses

JP:

JP:

JP:

JP: What time is the game tonight?

Carlos: Not sure. I can't go.

MORE TO THINK ABOUT

The questions below will help you to think more about how meaning can sometimes get confused through texts and online. Talk about this with a parent, relative, teacher, counselor, or other trustworthy adult. You can use the lines provided to jot down thoughts about each question.

1. How is talking online different from talßking face-to-face?

   _____

   _____

   _____

   _____

2. How could a text, post, photo, or online message be misunderstood by a reader? Give an example from your own life.

   _____

   _____

3. Do you think it is easier for someone to be cruel online than it is for them to be cruel in person?

   _____

4. Has there ever been a time when you misunderstood someone's online post? Did you think they were being mean when really they were trying to be funny?

   _____

5. Have you ever returned a cruel text with an ever crueler one? What happened?

   _____

   _____

ACTIVITY 19: THE STUDENT IS THE TEACHER

AS A KID, most of the time you are a student, learning from your teachers. Now, you get to be the teacher! That's right—what better way to learn even more about how to use technology in fun, safe, respectful ways than to teach these lessons to other kids?

THINK ABOUT IT

In this Activity, you will create a presentation. It will be fun, hands-on, interesting, informative, and, well, just plain **brilliant**. Plan to wow your audience with a lesson on **Tips for Stopping Cyberbullying**. Let your creative juices flow!

- You can choose to script a one-act play that shows kids standing up to cyberbullying
- You may design a poster with interesting facts and tips to stop online cruelty

  Better yet, consider ways that can you use technology to teach about technology!

- Create and share an anti-bullying video message for your peers. With your parent's permission, upload it to YouTube so that it can be viewed by an even wider audience.
- Put together a brief PowerPoint presentation to teach your classmates about cyberbullying.

Whatever format you use, this is your opportunity to make your world a better place by teaching others to use technology respectfully.

Use the Presentation Plan on the next page to map out your presentation.

TIPS FOR **STOPPING** CYBERBULLYING

Presentation Plan

Format: (circle one)   Video   Play   Poster   Other: _____

Who I will present to: _____

Who I will talk to about scheduling the presentation: _____

Presentation date: _____

Use the following checklist to be sure key ideas are included in your presentation:

☐ Define cyberbullying.

☐ Give examples of common devices that are used to hurt others online.

☐ Explain why cyberbullying is a problem for young people.

☐ List at least 5 things kids can do to use technology respectfully.

☐ List at least 5 things kids can do to deal with cyberbullying when they become aware of it.

☐ Give an example of something kind a kid could say to someone else who has been cyberbullied.

Presentation Planning Notes:

_____

_____

_____

_____

_____

_____

_____

_____

_____

_____

_____

_____

ACTIVITY 20: PLEDGE TO BE CYBERBULLYING FREE

IN THIS SECTION OF YOUR ACTIVITY BOOK, you have been thinking through all the fun ways to use technology safely and respectfully. You have been learning smart strategies for stopping online cruelty and cyberbullying. In the last Activity of this section, you will have the chance to put all of your new knowledge and skills together.

THINK ABOUT IT

A *pledge* is a way to say that you will follow certain rules or guidelines. On the next page, you'll find a pledge. It asks you to promise that when you use technology, you will be honorable, responsible, and kind. Read through each statement in the pledge. Consider how your use of smartphones, tablets, computers, video games, and other devices can change or improve, based on these rules. Are you ready to do your part to make technology a safe, fun way for kids to connect?

This pledge can be signed and kept inside this Activity Book. Or, you may carefully tear it out and place it somewhere you'll see it often. That way, the guidelines will stay fresh in your mind. Perhaps a class at school—or your entire school—will want to make a similar pledge. Ask a trustworthy teacher to share the pledge with a group of kids. You can all work together to keep online interactions respectful and fun.

I PLEDGE TO BE CYBERBULLYING FREE

1. I will text, share, and post only items that I consider kind and would be willing to say to someone in person.

2. I will always take time to think before I post my thoughts, responses, or photos, especially if I'm feeling angry or sad.

3. If I see cyberbullying, I will do whatever I can to stop it. I will not join in. I will not just ignore it. I know how to report cyberbullying and who to report it to.

4. I will use strong passwords and protect others' rights to privacy.

5. I will balance my time between online interactions and face-to-face friendships.

6. I will enjoy what technology has to offer in safe, respectful, kind ways at all times.

ADD YOUR OWN PROMISES HERE:

7. _____

_____

8. _____

_____

Signed: _____

Date: _____

Witness: _____

1. This pledge left you 2 open spaces to write in your own commitments to safe, respectful online interactions. If you had even more spaces, what would you have added?

_____

_____

2. Are there any commitments on the pledge that seem difficult to you? Which one(s)?

_____

_____

3. Who did you choose as your "Witness" to sign the pledge?

_____

- The purpose of having a Witness is to connect you with someone—maybe a friend, a family member, or a teacher—who can help you keep your pledge. That person can tell you if you have crossed a line into online cruelty or cyberbullying.

- All of us need a person in our lives who is honest enough to tell us when we have messed up and wise enough to help us make things right again.

Key 4: Be Cyberbullying Free

CHECKPOINT

1. What are some of your favorite ways to use technology? (Check all that apply.)

☐ Texting my friends

☐ Being able to watch whatever videos I want

☐ Being able to contact my friends easily when we're not at school

☐ Playing games

☐ Relaxing

☐ Finding information to help with school work

☐ Other: _____

2. What are some of the biggest risks and dangers of technology for you?
(Check all that apply.)

☐ People can post cruel comments, photos, and videos

☐ People can set up fake accounts on social media and games

☐ I care too much about what other people say about me online

☐ I feel like I'm not "good enough" if I don't get a lot of "likes" and followers

☐ Seeing what other people are doing online makes me feel like I'm missing out

☐ Seeing what other people are doing online makes me feel like my own life is boring

☐ Sometimes I get so caught up in technology that I don't get school work done

☐ Sometimes I get so caught up in technology that I don't get enough sleep

☐ Sometimes I spend more time on my gadget than I do with friends and family

☐ I worry about strangers that might try to contact me online

☐ Other: _____

3. Draw a line between each **Rule of Netiquette** and its correct explanation:

Choose your words carefully   Think before you post.

The Internet is not a weapon   Anytime you see cyberbullying, report it right away.

Take it slow   Never share private information online. This includes your full name, home address, photos, school name, and phone number.

Report it   If you wouldn't say something to a person's face, don't text it or post it online.

Don't talk to strangers   Don't gossip about people online or when you text.

4. Which of the following voices is best to use if you want to better understand someone's meaning in a text or online post? (Circle one.)

    a. A *Mean* voice

    b. A *Meek* voice

    c. A *Mean-It* voice

5. List 2 important **Tips for Stopping Cyberbullying**:

_____

_____

Key 4: Be Cyberbullying Free

✓ CHECKPOINT
ANSWER KEY

1. What are some of your favorite ways to use technology? (Check all that apply.)

2. What are some of the biggest risks and dangers of technology for you? (Check all that apply.)

For Questions 1 & 2, any answer that applies to you is a correct response!

3. Draw a line between each Rule of Netiquette and its correct explanation:

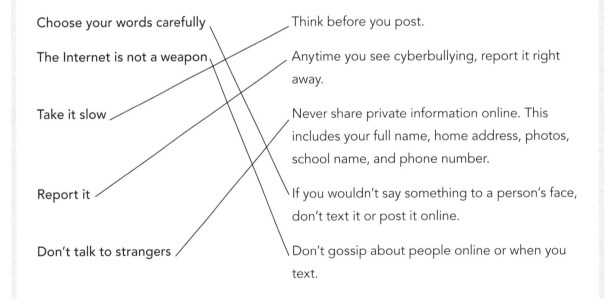

Choose your words carefully

The Internet is not a weapon

Take it slow

Report it

Don't talk to strangers

Think before you post.

Anytime you see cyberbullying, report it right away.

Never share private information online. This includes your full name, home address, photos, school name, and phone number.

If you wouldn't say something to a person's face, don't text it or post it online.

Don't gossip about people online or when you text.

4. Which of the following voices is best to use if you want to better understand someone's meaning in a text or online post? (Circle one.)

    a. A *Mean* voice

    b. A *Meek* voice

    (c.) A *Mean-It* voice

5. List 2 important **Tips for Stopping Cyberbullying**:

There are many possible correct answers to this question. Sample tips include:

1. Don't share your password with anyone but a parent.
2. Report cyberbullying anytime you see it.
3. If you wouldn't say it to someone's face, don't say it online.
4. Think before you post, especially if you are feeling angry, sad, or frustrated.
5. Don't allow others to take photos or videos that could be used in an embarrassing way.

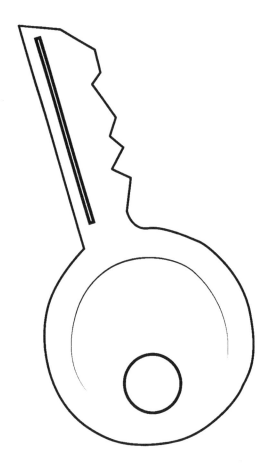

KEY 4: *I am cyberbullying free!*

LEVEL-UP YOUR SKILLS TO HANDLE BULLYING

ACTIVITY 21: THIS IS MY BRAIN ON BULLYING

DID YOU KNOW that your brain is designed to handle bullying? Every human being has both an "emotional" and a "logical" part of their brain. Each part gives you the chance to *choose* how you respond to bullying. In this Activity, you will learn how your amazing brain gives you the power to make wise decisions. It will help you make good choices whenever you encounter bullying.

THINK ABOUT IT

Make a fist* with your hand. Now, fold your thumb into your palm and bend your fingers over it. Believe it or not, this is a pretty close model of your brain! In this activity, we will talk about 3 parts of your amazing brain:

1. Your wrist is like the **brain stem**—the part of your brain that connects to your spinal cord. (Your arm is like the spinal cord.) The brain stem controls things that keep you alive, such as your heart rate and breathing.

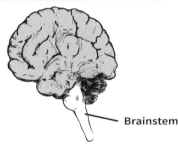

Brainstem

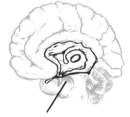

Limbic system

2. Your thumb is like the **limbic system**—the part of your brain that helps you feel your feelings. That is why it is often called your "emotional brain." When you feel sudden anger or sadness after being bullied, your limbic system is working!

* The hand model of the brain is adapted from Siegel, D. (2012). Dr. Daniel Siegel presenting a hand model of the brain [Video file]. Retrieved from https://www.youtube.com/watch?v=gm9CIJ74Oxw

KEY POINT: FIGHT, FLIGHT, OR FREEZE

Together, the brain stem and limbic system control your body's *fight, flight, or freeze response*. This is how your body handles stress, no matter what caused it. It happens whether a shark is about to bite you with his teeth or a classmate is about to bully you with his words. For example:

- When someone says something cruel, you might *freeze* up and not know what to do or say.
- When a classmate hits you, you might *fight* back without even thinking.
- When your friends leave you out, you might run away from the room. Another way to say "run away" is *flight*.

These sudden responses mean that your brain stem and limbic system have taken charge of your body!

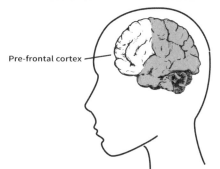

Pre-frontal cortex

3. The front part of your fingers, when wrapped over your thumb, are like the **pre-frontal cortex.** This part of your brain helps you make good decisions. It is also known as your **"logical brain"** because it lets you stop and think before doing what your brain stem and limbic system tell you to do.

This is very important. When bullying happens, you can THINK about your choices for how to respond. Then you can CHOOSE the best decision. Even in bad situations, you can make something good happen.

The Brain Stem, Limbic System, and Pre-frontal Cortex

HERE IS A DIAGRAM OF THE HUMAN BRAIN. It shows the brain stem, limbic system, and pre-frontal cortex. Using the information you have just read, complete the following activity.

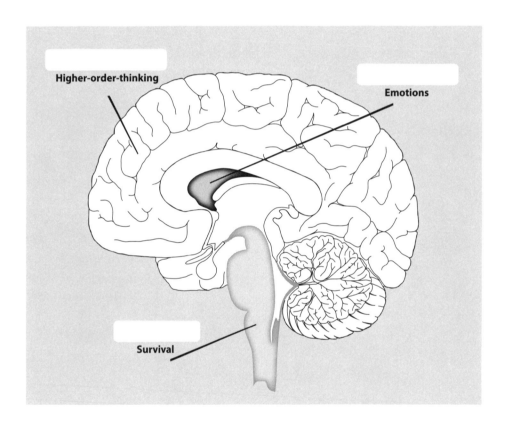

Higher-order-thinking

Emotions

Survival

1. In the boxes provided, label the **brain stem**, **limbic system**, and **pre-frontal cortex**.

2. Draw a line to match each part of the brain with what it does:

    a. Brain stem   **1.** Emotional thinking

    b. Limbic system   **2.** Logical thinking

    c. Pre-frontal cortex   **3.** Controls heart rate, breathing

3. Lightly shade each section of the brain as follows:
    *   Brain stem = blue
    *   Limbic system = red
    *   Pre-frontal cortex = green

MORE TO THINK ABOUT

What does all of this brain science have to do with bullying?
Whenever someone is cruel to you, your brain is busy!

*   Your face might get red and feel hot. This is because of what's going on in your brain stem.
*   You may feel angry, embarrassed, or sad. This is because of what's going on in your limbic system.

These parts of your brain, when left on their own, may cause you to hit, cry, yell, or do something else that is not nice. It might feel good at the time, but it will make your problem worse.

- On the other hand, if you STOP and think when you notice bullying, you allow your pre-frontal cortex to take control of the other parts of your brain. In doing so, you gain a very important power—*the ability to THINK through your choices and choose the best response.*

In Activity 13, you learned that you always have choices about how to respond to conflict and bullying. **Your pre-frontal cortex is the part of your brain that gives you the ability to choose helpful responses.**

In the next Activity, you will read real-life bullying scenes. Then you will decide if the response to the scene is caused by "emotional brain" reacting or "logical brain" responding.

The Brain Stem, Limbic System, and Pre-frontal Cortex

A N S W E R   K E Y

1. In the boxes provided, label the **brain stem**, **limbic system**, and **pre-frontal cortex**.

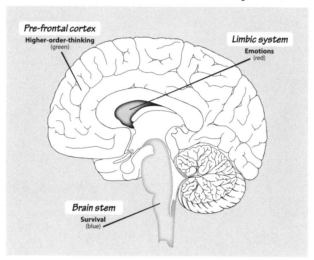

2. Draw a line to match each part of the brain with what it does:

   a. Brain stem   **1.** Emotional thinking

   b. Limbic system   **2.** Logical thinking

   c. Pre-frontal cortex   **3.** Controls heart rate, breathing

3. Lightly shade each section of the brain as follows:

   - Brain stem = blue
   - Limbic system = red
   - Pre-frontal cortex = green

ACTIVITY 22: WHICH BRAIN ARE YOU USING?

IN THE LAST ACTIVITY, you learned about 3 parts of your amazing brain. You learned how your *pre-frontal cortex* gives you the power to make good choices when you face bullying. In this Activity, you'll read about 5 real-life situations. You will figure out if they were handled with "emotional brain thinking" or "logical brain thinking."

THINK ABOUT IT

Anytime you need to remember how your amazing brain works, just make a fist! Your wrist, thumb, and 4 folded fingers can show you the most important parts of your brain's response to bullying and stress. To review:

a. Brain stem   **1.** Emotional thinking

b. Limbic system   **2.** Logical thinking

c. Pre-frontal cortex   **3.** Controls heart rate, breathing

WHICH BRAIN?

Directions:

Read each of the situations below. Decide if the response to it is an emotional, limbic system reaction or a thoughtful response by the pre-frontal cortex.

Situation 1:

Mrs. Wagner is handing back the math tests from last week. Kristy gets hers and sees that she made many mistakes. She scored a 5/10 on her test and is very upset. Emily leans over Kristy's desk and yells, "Whadya get? Whadya get?" Kristy is so embarrassed that she yells, "Go away, Emily! It's none of your stupid business!"

Circle which part of her brain Kristy is using to respond to Emily:

Limbic system   Pre-frontal cortex

Situation 2:

Grace and Connor are chosen by the gym teacher to be team captains for kickball. Silas is excited because Connor is his best friend and he thinks Connor will pick him first. Connor doesn't pick Silas first, however. Neither does Grace. In fact, Silas is the very last kid in the whole 3rd grade to be picked for kickball. He is embarrassed and wants to hide. As he walks toward the field with his team, Silas takes a deep breath. He says to himself, "You're going to go out there and play the best game of your life so that next time, you'll be picked first."

Circle which part of his brain Silas is using to respond to being chosen last:

Limbic system   Pre-frontal cortex

Situation 3:

On the bus ride to school, Pete and Cooper make fun of Dawson for wearing his big brother's old clothes. They taunt him for not having the new, name-brand sports gear that Pete and Cooper wear. Dawson looks at his 2 classmates like they are crazy. He says, "Whatever, dudes." Then he turns to the kid on his left and starts a conversation about football.

Circle which part of his brain Dawson is using to respond to being teased:

Limbic system   Pre-frontal cortex

Situation 4:

Every time Charlotte plays with Kayla, Lucy tells her, "Why are you playing with Kayla? You don't even want to be my friend anymore!" Every time Charlotte plays with Lucy, Kayla says, "I won't be your friend anymore if you keep playing with Lucy." Charlotte feels torn because she wants to be friends with *both* girls. The next time Lucy and Kayla ask her to choose sides, Charlotte says in a *Mean-It* voice, "I do want to be your friend. I don't want to fight with you." Then she goes to find a different group of friends to play with at recess.

Circle which part of her brain Charlotte is using to stop this friendship drama:

Limbic system   Pre-frontal cortex

Situation 5:

Gianna and Kessie are texting back and forth one night about Kessie's crush on Lucas. Kessie tells Gianna she is thinking about asking Lucas to the dance. The next day in school, Gianna gets mad at Kessie for not saving her a seat at their lunch table. She takes out her phone, copies the texts where Kessie talks about liking Lucas, and posts them online for their whole 7th-grade class to see.

Circle which part of her brain Gianna is using to get back at Kessie for not saving her a seat:

Limbic system   Pre-frontal cortex

MORE TO THINK ABOUT

In the space below, draw your own comic strip that shows either an *emotional* brain reaction or a *logical* brain response. For added fun, challenge a friend, parent, relative, or teacher to read your cartoon. See if they can tell you which part of the brain is at work.

Circle which part of the brain was used to respond: Limbic system   Pre-frontal cortex

WHICH BRAIN?

ANSWER KEY

Situation 1: Limbic system

Kristy is feeling upset over her grade. When Emily yells, "Whadya get? Whadya get?" Kristy shoves Emily and speaks to her rudely. Kristy's emotional brain, or limbic system, gets the best of her in this situation.

   If something like this happens again, Kristy should STOP to THINK a moment, take a deep breath, and calmly say to Emily in a *Mean-It* voice, "Please give me some space, Emily. I don't like to show my grades to other people."

Situation 2: Pre-frontal cortex

Silas feels embarrassed at being picked last by his friend, Connor, who he thought would pick him first. Instead of reacting in a negative way, however, he makes the CHOICE to breathe deeply and say encouraging words to himself to stay calm.

Situation 3: Pre-frontal cortex

No one likes to be teased about what they are wearing. However, instead of showing Pete and Cooper that he is upset, Dawson CHOOSES to act like their teasing doesn't bother him. He gives them a *Mean-It* response. Then he turns his focus to kids who are nicer.

Situation 4: Pre-frontal cortex

It's very difficult to feel caught between friends. Charlotte finds herself in a very common situation, in which friends are trying to control who she is (and is not) friends with. Charlotte is too smart and too powerful to let others control her, however. She CHOOSES NOT TO CHOOSE between Lucy and Kayla and finds other friends to play with at recess.

Situation 5: Limbic system

Gianna's feelings are hurt when Kessie does not save her a seat at lunch. She uses her smartphone to get back at Kessie.

   Next time Gianna gets overwhelmed by her feelings, she should TAKE IT SLOW before posting anything online that could hurt her friend. In a moment of anger, Gianna may have lost a friend forever.

ACTIVITY 23: ARE YOU A DUCK OR A SPONGE?

IN THE LAST 2 ACTIVITIES, you learned how your amazing brain deals with bullying. What you do when others treat you badly affects whether they keep treating you that way. In other words, *you are powerful!*

THINK ABOUT IT

For this activity, you will need:

- A rubber duck
- A dry sponge
- 2 cups, both full of water
- A sink

If you don't have these things handy, you will simply need your imagination.

Directions:

1. First, take the dry sponge. Think about how it feels in your hand. Below, circle the word that best describes its weight.

Heavy   Light

2. Next, hold the sponge in your hand, over the sink. With your other hand, slowly pour one of the cups of water onto the sponge. Try to cover the sponge with the water without spilling it into the sink.

3. Notice how the sponge has changed in response to having water poured over it. Circle the word that best describes its weight now.

Heavier   Lighter

4. Put the wet sponge aside.

5. Take the rubber duck in your hand. Hold it over the sink. Now pour the other cup of water over its back. Which statement best describes what happens to the water this time?

    a. The water sinks into the duck, just like it did the sponge.

    b. The water rolls right off the duck's back and into the sink.

6. Did the duck's weight changed in response to having water poured over it? Circle the word that best describes its weight now.

Heavier   Lighter   About the same

MORE TO THINK ABOUT

It's no secret that kids can be cruel. Sometimes, their words and actions—or even their silence—can feel like a cold bucket of water being dumped on your head. When this happens, it is helpful to remember that you have 2 basic **CHOICES**:

1. You can choose to act like a *sponge* that soaks up the hurt and becomes weighed down.

2. You can choose to act like a *duck* and let hurtful behaviors roll off your back as you keep on swimming.

It's not always easy to act like a duck. Hurtful actions by others are not easy to ignore. There *is* an important time and place to show your true feelings about being bullied. *But the heat of the moment is never the right time.*

KEY POINT

One thing we know about kids who bully is that they want to get a big reaction from their targets. When they see that they can hurt someone and make them feel heavy and weighed down, they feel **P**owerful. When they feel powerful, they are more likely to bully again and again.

On the other hand, when you show that you can laugh it off in the moment and just keep on going about your day, you don't give away any of your power. The person who tried to bully you will be more likely to move on. He or she now knows you are too strong to be bullied.

Make it a habit to "act like a duck" whenever you face bullying.

WRITE ABOUT IT

Tell about a time when you, or someone you know, acted like a sponge in the face of bullying. What happened in the moment? What happened later?

_____

_____

_____

_____

_____

_____

Tell about a time when you, or someone you know, acted like a duck in the face of bullying. What happened in the moment? What happened later?

_____

_____

_____

_____

_____

_____

ACTIVITY 24: QUIZ TIME:
WHAT IS YOUR CHILL OUT LEVEL (COL)?

WHILE IT'S NATURAL to get weighed down (and feel like a sponge) during a conflict or to want to strike back at people who have hurt you, you have learned in this Activity Book that reacting in anger almost always makes situations worse. In this Activity, you'll learn ways to keep calm, *chill out*, and swim like a duck when bullying happens.

THINK ABOUT IT

Most kids can name the things that make them feel upset. But many don't know how to chill out when they are stressed. How do you relax after a fight with a friend? What makes you feel calm after reading a mean post online or finding out that your friends all went to a party without you?

The next game will help you find your Chill Out Level (COL). You will learn ways to stay calm when bullying and other stressful things happen. Remember: Your pre-frontal cortex (*logical brain*) can do its job only when you stay calm and cool!

What's Your COL?

KEEP CALM AND STOP BULLYING

Directions: PART 1:

First, use the space below to think of ideas for keeping calm after a stressful incident with a friend. Write down as many ways as you can think of.

My List of Ways to CHILL OUT:

1. *Take 5 deep breaths.*
2. _____
3. _____

4. _____
5. _____
6. _____

Next, use the lines below to challenge someone else to write down their answers to the same question: "How do you chill out after a stressful incident with a friend?" Lines are provided so that their answers can be written in your book.

A Friend's List of Ways to CHILL OUT:

1. *Have a drink of water.*
2. _____
3. _____

4. _____
5. _____
6. _____

Scoring for PART 1:

a. Give yourself **1** point for every idea you came up with.

b. Give yourself **2** extra points for every idea you thought of that was not on the other person's list.

c. Tally your score. Write it in the space marked "My COL Score So Far."

My COL Score so Far: _____

PART 2:

Check out the list of ways to chill out on the next page, then turn to page 137 for final scoring directions.

50 WAYS FOR KIDS TO **CHILL OUT**

1. Go for a walk

2. Talk to an adult you can trust

3. Take 5 deep breaths

4. Squeeze a stress ball

5. Count to 10 slowly

6. Count backward from 10

7. Blow bubbles

8. Have a drink of water

9. Talk about it with a good friend

10. Ask for a hug from a friend

11. Pet a friendly animal

12. Hug a stuffed animal

13. Draw

14. Color

15. Hum a tune softly

16. Sing your favorite song in your head

17. Listen to music

18. Stop and think before saying or doing anything

19. Find a way to laugh about what happened

20. Spend some time outside

21. Practice yoga

22. Bounce a ball

23. Throw a ball

24. Go for a run

25. Think of happy or funny things

26. Remind yourself that it's OK to be upset

27. Remind yourself that it's never OK to hurt others

28. Say to yourself, "I can handle this"

29. Write about what is bothering you

30. Write a letter to someone you love

31. Read a good book

32. Do something kind for someone else

33. Go to a quiet place

34. Pray

35. Wrap yourself in a warm blanket

36. Take a warm shower

37. Relax the muscles in your face

38. Touch something soft or smooth

39. Smell something vanilla or lavender

40. Taste something yummy

41. Listen to the silence

42. Look at a photo of a loved one

43. Take a nap

44. Say "I love you" to someone special

45. Say the alphabet slowly

46. Let sand flow slowly between your fingers

47. Crumple paper

48. Eat a crunchy snack

49. Drink a cup of tea

50. Be proud of yourself for choosing a smart response!

Final Scoring Instructions:

1. Read through the list of **50** Ways for Kids to **CHILL OUT**.
2. Give yourself **5** points for each idea on your list that is not included in the **50** Ways for Kids to **CHILL OUT**.
3. Write down your score below, then try to answer the Bonus Question before learning your COL.

COL Score Now: _____

QUESTION:

What do all the **50** Ways for Kids to **CHILL OUT** have in common? Write your answer in the space provided:

_____

_____

_____

The answer to the Bonus Question can be found at the end of this activity. Check it out now, then return to this page to write down your Final Score in the space below.

My Final COL Score _____

What Is My COL?

Use your Final Score to determine your COL:

0–5 points: CUP OF TEA

You are learning to take time to calm down. This will help you to respond well to bullying and other stressful situations. Keep exploring new ways to *chill out* and cool down.

6–20 points: COLD LEMONADE

You know lots of ways to chill out and calm your brain. Because of this, you have many good choices for responding to bullying. Add any new ideas from the list of ways to *chill out* to your list of skills. This way, you will always be prepared to handle bullying.

Consider using what you know to help other kids deal with bullying. Whenever you see kids being cruel, step in to stop it. Encourage the other kids to keep a cool head and choose helpful responses.

20+ points: FROZEN SMOOTHIE ON THE BEACH

You know how to stay cool as a cucumber, no matter what kinds of bullying you face. Adults know they can count on you to stay calm and make good choices when you are stressed. Kids look up to you because you never seem to let your feelings get the best of you. Kids who bully avoid picking on you because they know that you don't allow them to have power over you.

Being respected by others is a privilege, so use your power wisely. Speak up for others who are being bullied. (See more on how to do this later in your Activity Book!) Be an example of showing kindness to everyone, every day.

WRITE ABOUT IT

Think about a time when you were the target of bullying. It may have been physical, verbal, relational bullying, or cyberbullying. In the space below, write down a plan for how you could relax and keep calm if this happened again. Include as many ways to chill out as you can. Give details.

After you have made your plan, share it with a friend, parent, or trusted adult. Ask that person to help you stick to your plan anytime bullying happens. It is helpful to connect with someone who can stay calm and help you use your logical brain. Two heads are better than one!

_____

_____

_____

_____

_____

_____

_____

_____

_____

⫸BONUS QUESTION ANSWER

All of the **50** Ways for Kids to **CHILL OUT** have one thing in common:
They give your amazing brain time to STOP AND THINK. Using your logical brain will help you make good choices when you respond to bullying.

Give yourself **10** additional points if you got the Bonus Question correct!

ACTIVITY 25: FRIENDSHIP EMOJIS ☺

DO YOU LOVE FINDING the perfect emoji to describe a feeling to a friend? An old saying goes, *A picture is worth a thousand words*. We all know that sometimes a picture says it best. This is true when it comes to feelings about bullying.

THINK ABOUT IT

Below is a list of 7 "feeling words." They describe emotions often felt by kids who have been bullied. For each one, draw your own emoji that expresses the feeling behind the word.

FEELING WORD	EMOJI
ANGRY	
CONFUSED	
LONELY	
EMBARRASSED	
INVISIBLE	
SAD	
SCARED	

The words listed in the activity on page 140 are just a start! There is no end to the emotions you might feel about being bullied.

KEY POINT

The first step in dealing with emotions is to name them. *Naming feelings is very important. Any time we use language to describe emotions, we move them from our emotional brain to our logical brain. This way, we gain control over them.*

In the space below, make your own list of words to describe feelings you have had. Think about how you have felt with healthy friendships as well as with bullying. For each word, create an emoji to represent the feeling.

FEELING WORD	EMOJI

ACTIVITY 26: WHAT TO DO WHEN A FRIENDSHIP IS OVER

BEST FRIENDS FOREVER. BFF. Have you ever used this phrase with a friend? The friendships you have in elementary and middle school can be a lot of fun. You might feel so close to someone that you have a hard time imagining ever *not* being friends. But, just like you are growing and changing every day, so is your friend. Sometimes kids grow together; sometimes they grow apart. When it comes to childhood friendships, the only thing that stays the same is change.

This might sound scary to you right now. The truth, though, is that *you are strong enough* to handle whatever happens in your friendships. What's more, *you are smart enough* to know when a friendship is no longer close or fun. In this Activity, you'll learn to value the best parts of a friendship. You will also learn how to move on—when the time is right—with grace and dignity.

THINK ABOUT IT

Has your BFF ever "forgotten" to save you a seat on the bus? Has your friend tackled you extra hard in football or thrown a ball right at your face? As you learned at the beginning of this Activity Book, there are times when friends are rude. There may even be days when they are very mean. But it's different when these actions become a **P**attern of ugliness. It's important to know when to say to yourself, "Enough is enough. I deserve better." Sometimes you need to end the friendship for your own well-being.

This is easier said than done! First of all, it's confusing when the person who used to be your best friend is now treating you badly. Most of us are quick to give our BFFs a second and third (and fourth and fifth and eleventh) chance. We're usually all pretty slow to admit to ourselves that things aren't getting any better. Also, it's really embarrassing to be ignored, taunted, and hurt by the person you counted on to pay attention to, include, laugh with, and have fun with you. Throw in feelings of anger, loneliness, and maybe fear—and you've got a really tough situation!

ADVICE NEEDED!

If you have ever struggled to figure out which is worse—staying with a friendship or leaving it—then you are not alone!

Directions:
Read the real-life stories of kids looking for advice on what to do when a friend becomes a "frenemy." Then, read the advice given to the kids by trustworthy adults. Finally, add your words of wisdom on how to end the friendships with dignity.

Situation 1:

Jonny, Jake, and Ethan have known each other since they were in preschool. They were best friends throughout elementary school. In middle school, however, they started growing apart. Jake and Ethan were starters on the football team. Jonny only got playing time during the second half, if his team was already winning. Jake and Ethan never invited Jonny over anymore.

At the beginning of the school year, Jake and Ethan teased Jonny in a funny way about keeping the bench warm in football. By November, the teasing started to get more cruel and embarrassing. Jake and Ethan got everyone on their team to call Jonny "Waterboy," since he was more likely to get water for the players than to play on the field. When Jonny confronted them about getting everyone to call him "Waterboy," Jake said, "Dude, relax. It was just a joke! No one knew you'd be such a loser about it."

Jonny had never felt so alone. His older brother noticed how upset Jonny was one night and asked him about it. Jonny told him what had been going on all fall. This is what his brother told him:

BROTHER: Listen, bro. Friendships in middle school can be rough! Everyone says it's the girls that are so awful, but believe me—the guys can be just as bad. It stinks that this is happening to you, but I'm really glad that you finally told me about it because trying to handle this all alone is even worse. I've been through things like this with my friends, and I've got your back with Ethan and Jake.

JONNY: Thanks, dude. I know I probably sound really stupid, but I just don't get what I ever did to them.

BROTHER: If you did do something to them, they should tell you what it was and not just treat you like this. Friends don't just ditch friends without giving them a chance to hash it out. I'll bet you didn't do anything at all—it's just Jake and Ethan trying to climb up the school social ladder and pushing you down on their way up. It doesn't say anything bad about you, but it does tell you a lot about them. You know what I mean?

JONNY: I guess. But why now? We've been friends forever.

BROTHER: Trying to figure out other people's reasons for doing things is hopeless. Jake and Ethan might not even know why they're doing what they are doing. Let's just figure out what you can do to make your own situation better and not worry too much about them.

JONNY: OK. So, what should I do?

BROTHER: First, let me tell you what you shouldn't do! Never let Jake and Ethan get you upset in front of other people. No matter what they say, try to keep your cool and laugh things off. When they call you "Waterboy," come up with something funny to say back instead of getting mad. They're looking for a reaction from you. When they don't get one, they'll get bored and move on.

JONNY: Yeah, but it's so embarrassing. I hate it when they call me that!

BROTHER: I know that and you know that, and it's OK to hate the name. But you've gotta show them that you're not vulnerable to what they're saying. Be strong and confident in front of them. Laugh things off. Act like you could care less about what they say. It'll make all the difference, I promise you.

JONNY: OK, what else?

BROTHER: So, the other thing that works for me is just staying really positive. Keep your distance from Jake and Ethan when you can. Try to focus on the kids in your classes. Have you met any cool people to hang out with in any of your classes?

JONNY: Yeah, there is a pretty cool girl in homeroom named Aimee and a few guys in football that I knew from my old team.

BROTHER: Perfect. Here's my advice for you:

- Eat lunch with Aimee sometimes.
- Hang out with the other guys at football.
- When Ethan and Jake do approach you, look them in the eye so they know you are strong.
- Talk to them in a calm voice.
- Resist the urge to show them you're upset. Don't lose eye contact, agree with their put-downs, or insult them back.

- Try to find something funny to say.
- As soon as they start to be mean, change the subject or walk away.
- Focus on the kids who make you feel good about yourself.
- Move on from Ethan and Jake without sinking to their level.

What other advice would you give Jonny about handling Jake and Ethan?

_____

_____

Situation 2:

STUDENT: I invited Nikki to my party. As soon as she got there, she started making fun of everyone and everything. She told me that one of the other girls I invited was a loser. She said that I'd better be careful or people would start thinking I was a loser too. She said my dress was "hideous." I explained that my mother had made it and that I didn't like it much either but felt I had to wear it. She started telling everyone I was too poor to buy clothes. She was bossing me around, and when I wouldn't do what she told me to do, she started texting another friend of ours, telling her how lame my party was.

COUNSELOR: It never feels good to be let down by another person. We care about our friendships. It can feel so good to belong that sometimes we don't even realize that a friend is no longer good for us. It took real courage for you to talk to me about what happened. I am proud of you.

STUDENT: Thanks. I thought you were going to tell me to go back to class and handle it on my own. I guess this is all just really stupid.

COUNSELOR: Feelings are real. They are not stupid and you don't have to handle them on your own. It's important that you always surround yourself with people you can go to when you need help.

STUDENT: I am totally not talking to Nikki anymore!

COUNSELOR: What I want you to keep in mind is that the way you go about distancing yourself from Nikki is important and will say everything about the type of person you are. Here is some of my advice for you:

- Don't get into ugly wars of words with her, then half apologize by saying you were "just joking." That will only bring you down to her level.
- Resist the urge to talk badly about her to other friends—in person, online, by text, or in any way, shape, or form.
- In fact, don't put much of your energy on her at all. Shift your focus to what is going right in your life. Focus on the friendships and activities that make you feel good about yourself.
- Think about what you are doing and who you are with when you are your "best self," then plan your day accordingly. It might not be smooth sailing the whole way through, but if you keep it classy on your end, you'll free yourself up to find better friendships.

What other advice would you give this student about handling Nikki?

_____

_____

Situation 3:

Connor auditions for the school play and is offered a great role. Rehearsals are scheduled for every day after school, so Connor has to choose between hanging out with his friends and accepting the role. He chooses to do the play. Almost right away, his friends start making fun of him. They say things like, "So, are you going to have to wear tights for your role, Romeo?" and "Acting is so gay. Why do you want to be in a gay play? Are you gay or something?" Connor laughs at first, then tells the guys to "knock it off." But when one friend writes the word "gay" on his locker, Connor has had it.

What advice would you give Connor? (*Suggestions are provided at the end of the Activity.*)

_____

_____

WRITE ABOUT IT

In the space below, write about a real-life bullying situation that you know about or are involved in.

_____

_____

_____

_____

_____

_____

_____

_____

_____

_____

_____

_____

_____

_____

_____

- Share this situation with a trustworthy friend or adult. Ask for their advice on how to handle it.
- Talk over various options. Consider the pros and cons of each one.
- If you are involved in the situation, make a plan for how you will use the advice in your real life.
- Set a date to check back in with the friend or adult on how the advice worked out.

DISCUSSION OF **SITUATION 3**

Connor:

A very common way that boys (and some girls) put each other down is to use the word "gay" as an insult. It is very important that Connor knows that this type of name-calling is not OK and that he does not have to handle it on his own. Anyone giving Connor advice should tell him to:

- Use a *Mean-It* response, such as, "It's not cool to use that word as an insult" or "Do you even know what 'gay' means?"
- Respond with a *Mean-It* phrase and strong voice. This is often enough to end anti-gay name-calling.
- Reach out to a trustworthy adult and report the bullying if the boys don't stop using the word "gay" as an insult. Most schools have rules against anti-gay bullying. Teachers get training on how to end this type of bullying without life getting worse for people like Connor.
- Focus on the new friends he is meeting in the theatre and enjoy being in the play. When he is surrounded by people who like the same things he does, Connor can feel good about himself and how he chooses to spend his time.

ACTIVITY 27: "I TOOK IT OUT ON SOMEONE WHO DIDN'T DESERVE IT"

HAVE YOU EVER HAD A FRIEND or family member take their bad mood out on you? Most of us have been in a situation where we got the bad end of someone else's anger or frustration. Maybe that person felt safe letting her emotions out on you. Maybe she knew you were likely to understand and forgive her. Either way, you probably know firsthand that it's no fun to be on the receiving end of someone else's outburst. In this Activity, you will learn more about how bad moods can travel.

THINK ABOUT IT

Think carefully: *Have you ever taken your bad mood or frustration out on someone who didn't deserve it?* Maybe you had a rough morning at home and took it out on some kid on the bus? Maybe school was terrible and you took it out on your little sister at home?

Let's face it: We've all misplaced a mood or two. But have you ever stopped to think about how your actions affect the person you are being cruel to? Or about how that person may then pass on his frustration to the next person he sees? *How many people are actually affected when emotions like anger and frustration are acted out?*

"IT ALL STARTED WITH BRIAN"

Directions:

Read "It All Started with Brian" below. Using the line of paper dolls, tell how each person in the story is affected by the actions of the last person in line.

"It All Started With Brian"

Brian made fun of Michelle for wearing a "loser shirt" to school. Michelle felt embarrassed. At lunch, Michelle took her feelings out on Tonya by not letting her sit with the group. Tonya sat alone and felt left out. On the bus ride home, Tonya ignored her little brother, Matthew, when he tried to sit down next to her. When their mother asked the kids how their day went, both kids brushed past her. Matthew shouted, "Just leave me alone!"

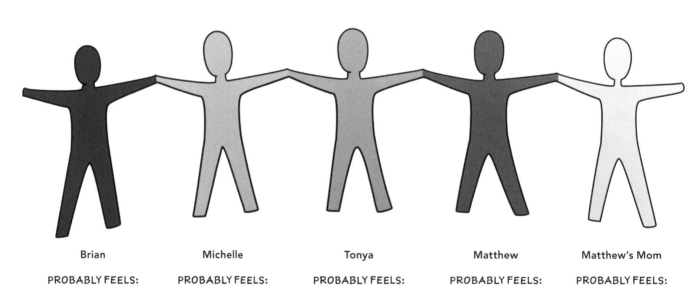

Brian	Michelle	Tonya	Matthew	Matthew's Mom
PROBABLY FEELS: GRUMPY	PROBABLY FEELS:	PROBABLY FEELS:	PROBABLY FEELS:	PROBABLY FEELS:

KEY POINT

In this situation, we don't know if Brian was taking a bad mood out on Michelle, if he was bullying Michelle, or if he was just trying to make a (lame) joke. What we do know, though, is that his spur-of-the-moment words had a lasting, bad impact on several other people! It's important for all of us to remember that *our words matter*—not only to the person we speak them to, but to others on down the line.

WRITE ABOUT IT

Use the paper dolls below to show a time when you said or did something hurtful to one person that caused a painful chain reaction.

 _____

_____

_____

_____

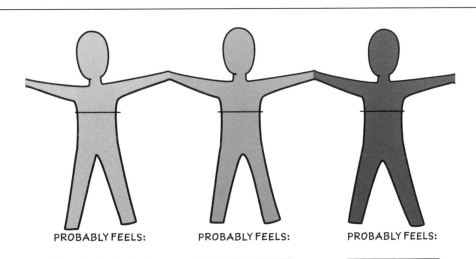

PROBABLY FEELS: PROBABLY FEELS: PROBABLY FEELS:

_____   _____   _____

ACTIVITY 28: TAKING A NEW POINT OF VIEW

HAVE YOU HEARD THE SAYING that *there are 2 sides to every story*? Every human being sees the world through their own eyes and from their own point of view. Because of this, it's common for 2 people to look at the exact same thing and see it completely differently. Willingness to see the world from someone else's point of view is a skill that builds friendships.

THINK ABOUT IT

In the space provided below, write down the type of animal you see when you look at the image on the next page:

I see a: _____

Now, look at the image again. Try to see a different animal in the image. Write down what you see in the space below:

I also see a: _____

If you are having trouble seeing a different animal, don't worry. It can be hard to see something new once your eyes have focused on the original animal. Ask a parent, sister, brother, or friend if they can help you see a different animal than the one you have written above. Once you have found it, you may move on to the next section.

WRITE ABOUT IT

Based on the picture on the last page:

1. Is this a picture of a duck? (Circle one.)   Yes   No

2. Is this a picture of a rabbit? (Circle one.)   Yes   No

3. How is it that both answers can be correct?

Explain: _____

_____

4. In the space below, draw a picture of a situation in which 2 people see something completely differently—and yet are both right.

5. How could being able to see from a new point of view help build a friendship? (Circle all that apply.)

   a. Kids like it when people listen to them and try to understand their point of view.

   b. Sometimes, being kind is more important than proving that you're right.

   c. Building a friendship is not as important as winning an argument with someone.

   d. When I listen to someone else's point of view, I can learn new and valuable things.

6. What is the best way to communicate with someone else when their point of view is different from yours? (Circle one.)

   a. Raise your voice until they know that your way is the only right way.

   b. Try to make the person feel stupid for their point of view.

   c. Ask the person questions about their point of view to try to learn more.

   d. Say nothing at all; everyone can have their own opinion.

Answers are given on the next page.

WRITE ABOUT IT

Based on the picture on page 152:

1. Is this a picture of a duck? (Circle one.) (Yes)   No

2. Is this a picture of a rabbit? (Circle one.) (Yes)   No

3. How is it that both answers can be correct? Explain:

Depending on how you look at the picture, it can show both a rabbit and a duck. Often, 2 people can see a situation completely differently and both be 100% correct.

4. In the space below, draw a picture of a situation in which 2 people see something completely differently—and yet are both right.

Any picture that shows at least 2 points of view about one thing is correct!

5. How could being able to see from a new point of view help build a friendship? (Circle all that apply.)

(**a.**) Kids like it when people listen to them and try to understand their point of view.

(**b.**) Sometimes, being kind is more important than proving that you're right,

c. Building a friendship is not as important as winning an argument with someone.

(**d.**) When I listen to someone else's point of view, I can learn new and valuable things.

6. What is the best way to communicate with someone else when their point of view is different from yours? (Circle one.)

a. Raise your voice until they know that your way is the only right way.

b. Try to make the person feel stupid for their point of view.

(**c.**) Ask the person questions about their point of view to try to learn more.

d. Say nothing at all; everyone can have their own opinion.

Key 5: Level-Up Your Skills to Handle Bullying

CHECKPOINT

1. Unscramble the terms below to reveal features of your amazing brain:

    a. abnir etms   _____ _____

    b. cmibil semsty   _____ _____

    c. epr-oartnlf ertxoc   ____-_____ _____

    d. gtfhi   _____

    e. ihflgt   _____

    f. erzeef   _____

    g. ollgica anibr   _____ _____

    h. nlaetmoio ainrb   _____ _____

2. Circle the ??? ?????? ??? ?ents th ?????? ?? ?????? bullying:

3. Which of the following is NOT one of the ways to *chill out* discussed in Activity 24? (Circle one.)

    a. Go for a run

    b. Count backward from 10

    c. Say to yourself, "I can handle this."

d. Take your bad mood out on your mother

4. When it comes to ending a friendship, which of the following is NOT a good idea? (Circle one.)

    a. Use a Mean-It voice to tell the person what they did that bothered you.

    b. Use the silent treatment to leave the person feeling hurt and confused.

    c. Spend time with friends you enjoy.

    d. Focus on activities that make you feel good about yourself.

5. Willingness to see the world from someone else's point of view is a skill that builds friendships. Is this statement true or false? (Circle one.)

        True   False

Key 5: Level-Up Your Skills to Handle Bullying

☑ CHECKPOINT

A N S W E R   K E Y

1. Unscramble the terms below to reveal features of your amazing brain:

   a. abnir etms   *brain stem*

   b. cmibil semsty   *limbic system*

   c. epr-oartnlf ertxoc   *pre-frontal cortex*

   d. gtfhi   *fight*

   e. ihflgt   *flight*

   f. erzeef   *freeze*

   g. ollgica anibr   *logical brain*

   h. nlaetmoio ainrb   *emotional brain*

2. Circle the picture below that represents the BETTER way to handle bullying:

3. Which of the following is NOT one of the ways to *chill out* discussed in Activity 24? (Circle one.)

   a. Go for a run

   b. Count backward from 10

   c. Say to yourself, "I can handle this."

   d. Take your bad mood out on your mother

4. When it comes to ending a friendship, which of the following is NOT a good idea? (Circle one.)

      a. Use a Mean-It voice to tell the person what they did that bothered you.

       Use the silent treatment to leave the person feeling hurt and confused.

      c. Spend time with friends you enjoy.

      d. Focus on activities that make you feel good about yourself.

5. Willingness to see the world from someone else's point of view is a skill that builds friendships. Is this statement true or false? (Circle one.)

            (True)   False

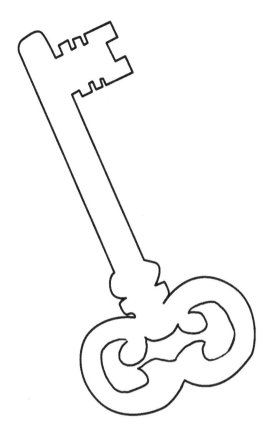

KEY 5: *I have leveled-up my skills to end bullying!*

KEY **6**

BE KNOWN
FOR BEING KIND

ACTIVITY 29: TEN THINGS TO SAY AND DO TO STOP BULLYING

DID YOU KNOW that bystanders are around during 9 out of every 10 cases of bullying? Are you aware that bystanders stand up for those being bullied less than 2 times out of 10?

Talk about a missed opportunity!

Studies show that when bystanders do step in, bullying usually stops within 10 seconds.

Talk about a chance to be someone's hero!

In this Activity, you will learn ways to stand up for anyone, anytime you see bullying. You will see how powerful you can be in making a difference in someone's life.

THINK ABOUT IT

Has a parent or teacher ever challenged you to stand up for a brother, sister, or classmate? Have you ever agreed that this would be a really great idea—if only you knew what to do or say?

If you answered yes to either question, you are not alone! Many kids say they'd like to stand up for people who are being bullied but don't know how. The good news is that standing up for others is probably a lot easier than you think! In fact, the simplest things you do are usually the best.

Below, you will find a list of 10 things that you can do to stop bullying anytime you see it. Then, you will add to the list by writing down simple actions and phrases to help a friend in need.

10 THINGS TO SAY AND DO TO **STOP BULLYING**

1. Stand with the person

Walk over and stand next to someone who is being bullied. Often, just being there can change the mood and stop the bullying. It also lets the person being bullied know that he is not alone.

2. Use a Mean-It statement

Say something like, "Cut it out, dude—that's not cool," in a *Mean-It* voice.

3. Change the subject

Stop bullying in its tracks by changing the subject. For example, ask if someone knows the date of the math test or the score of the football game.

4. Scatter the crowd

Say something like, "Guys, we've gotta get to class before the bell rings." This is a quick and easy way to stop bullying on the spot.

5. Show kindness

If you can't stop the bullying in the moment, talk to the person later that day. Invite her to hang out with you at lunch or sit with you on the bus.

6. Use humor

Try to lower the stress of a bullying situation by making kids laugh. Just make sure they are not laughing at the person being bullied!

7. Be a connector

Connect a person who gets bullied with an older kid who will be his friend and tell other kids not to pick on him.

8. Get help

Reach out to a trustworthy adult who will stop the bullying

9. Reach out

Reach out to a kid you saw being bullied. Tell her you are sorry about what happened to her.

10. Be a friend

Tell the kid being bullied that he is awesome and doesn't deserve to be treated badly. This simple act of friendship can make a big difference to him.

Now, it's your turn to add to the list. How can you show kindness and support to someone who is being bullied? In the space below, think of at least 2 more ways that you can step in to stop bullying and stand up for someone who needs a hero.

_____

_____

KEY POINT

Many kids don't know how and when to stand up for someone who is being bullied. This Activity Book is designed to give you skills to safely help others and stop bullying anytime you see it.

In this Activity, you learned 10 Things to Say and Do to Stop Bullying. In the next 3 Activities, you will learn more about WHAT to say, WHEN to say it, and HOW to become known for being kind.

ACTIVITY 30: BEFORE, DURING, AND AFTER WAYS TO STOP BULLYING

IN THE LAST ACTIVITY, you learned many ways to stand up for someone being bullied. You also learned that stopping bullying does not have to be hard. Rather, the simplest things you say and do can make the biggest difference. In this Activity, you'll take your new skills to the next level. You will learn about the *timing* of your actions.

THINK ABOUT IT

Have you ever felt badly that you missed your chance to stop bullying? Maybe you didn't change the subject when a kid was being picked on in the locker room. Or maybe you didn't make space at the lunch table for someone who was being left out. If so, cheer up! *There is no bad time to stand up for someone who is being bullied.*

Anytime is better than no time when it comes to showing kindness.

In the next few pages, you will read 3 bullying situations. For each case, you will think about what you could do before, during, and after to help the person being bullied.

Before, During, and After Ways You Can Help

Directions:

Read each real-life situation below. Write down at least 3 things that you could do to be a hero to the person being bullied. Challenge yourself to come up with an idea that can be used:

1. **Before** the bullying in order to prevent it
2. **During** the bullying to stop it on the spot
3. **After** the bullying to support and comfort the person who is bullied.

Situation 1: Jessie & Kris

Jessie is mad at Kris. She thinks Kris has been flirting with her boyfriend. Jessie doesn't want to say anything to Kris about it because she doesn't want to fight. Instead, Jessie makes a fake website about Kris. She uses all sorts of embarrassing photos and posts. Jessie gets other kids to post videos on Kris's wall. They all post about how they hate Kris and what a loser she is. In no time, the whole school seems to know about it.

WHAT COULD YOU DO TO HELP KRIS?

Before: _____

During: _____

After: _____

Situation 2: Darrell & the Bus Kids

Darrell dreads his bus ride home from middle school. Every day, the kids who sit behind him slap him on the back of his head. The kids who sit in front of him turn around to shout bad words. They tease him, asking, "What are you gonna do, cry to your mama?" One kid threatened to beat him down if he told anyone at school about what happens on the bus. Darrell has tried to get his parents to drive him home from school. They both work and can't change their schedule. This has been happening for months.

WHAT COULD YOU DO TO HELP DARRELL?

Before: _____

During: _____

After: _____

Situation 3: Chloe & Olivia

Chloe and Olivia have been best friends since kindergarten. In 3rd grade, they are put in different classes. Each girl makes new friends. All is fine at the beginning of the school year. But then, later in the year, Chloe starts to say things to Olivia like, "You're not my best friend anymore" and "You can't sit with me at lunch. This table is only for my new friends." One day, Olivia walks into the school cafeteria and finds that no one in the whole grade will sit with her. Everywhere she tries to put her tray down, kids say the same thing: "This table is only for cool kids. You are not one of them."

WHAT COULD YOU DO TO HELP OLIVIA?

Before: _____

During: _____

After: _____

Before, During, and After Ways You Can Help

A N S W E R   K E Y

There are many ways to stand up for kids before, during, and after bullying. Compare the ideas below with the ones you wrote down. Remember that you can always CHOOSE how you respond to bullying. Make yourself known for being someone who always chooses kindness.

SITUATION 1: JESSIE & KRIS

BEFORE:

- Refuse to post embarrassing videos or rude comments.
- Alert a teacher.
- Warn Kris about what is happening so she can stop it before it spreads further.
- Prevent the problem by telling Jessie that Kris is not flirting with her boyfriend.
- Encourage Jessie to talk to Kris and tell her why she is mad.

DURING:

- Take screen shots of the cyberbullying. Report it to an adult.
- Remind Jessie that what she is doing could get her in a lot of legal trouble.
- Tell Jessie that the website she made is not funny. Tell her to take it down right away.
- Refuse to take part in the cyberbullying.
- Tell others not to take part in the cyberbullying.
- Reach out to Kris as a friend. It is likely that she is feeling ganged up on and alone.

AFTER:

- Be there as a friend for Kris.
- Include Kris in activities and at your lunch table.
- Encourage Kris to get an adult's help.
- Offer to go with Kris to talk to a teacher, school counselor, or parent.

SITUATION 2: DARRELL & THE BUS KIDS

BEFORE:

- Invite Darrell to sit with you on the bus.
- Sit with Darrell near the front of the bus, closer to the driver.
- Talk to the bus driver in private to let him or her know what is happening.
- Request assigned seats on the bus to protect Darrell from the kids who are bullying him.
- Ask your parents to talk to Darrell's parents about what is happening on the bus.
- Tell a trustworthy teacher at school about what is happening to Darrell on the bus.

DURING:

- Use a Mean-It voice to tell the kids on the bus to "knock it off."
- Make your voice loud enough to get the bus driver's attention.
- Sit with Darrell on the bus. Help him to laugh or play a game.
- Ask a respected older student to sit with Darrell on the bus.

AFTER:

- Call Darrell after school. Tell him you are sorry about the way the other kids treat him.
- Tell Darrell that he does not deserve to be treated that way.
- Remind Darrell that you like him.
- Arrange for a group of nice kids to sit with Darrell on the bus ride from now on.
- If your parents ever drive you to school, offer Darrell a ride.
- Talk to a trustworthy teacher at school who can help address the situation.

SITUATION 3: CHLOE & OLIVIA

BEFORE:

- Refuse to go along with the crowd that is being cruel to Olivia.
- Tell Chloe and the other girls that what they are doing to Olivia is not cool.
- Get a bunch of your nicest friends to sit with you and Olivia during lunch.
- When you hear Chloe's plan to leave Olivia out at lunch, make up a believable reason to sit at a different table that day. Save a seat for Olivia at that table.

DURING:

- Refuse to go along with activities that exclude Olivia.
- Make a joke out of Chloe's statement that "only cool kids" sit at the lunch table. Use humor to distract everyone while making space for Olivia to sit.
- Start a new conversation at the table. Talk about a school event, holiday, or any subject that distracts from Chloe's cruel plans.
- In a Mean-It voice, tell the mean girls at lunch that "cools kids don't treat people that way."

AFTER:

- Talk to a teacher or lunch aide about the way Olivia is being treated.
- Text Olivia after school. Invite her to hang out with you and your friends.
- Help Olivia think of some Mean-It comebacks she could use next time Chloe and the other girls are cruel.

THINK ABOUT IT

Think about a time when you witnessed bullying. In the spaces below, draw at least one helpful thing you could have done Before, During, and After the event to be a hero to the person being bullied.

BEFORE

DURING

AFTER

ACTIVITY 31: 50 KIND WORDS AND PHRASES TO STOP BULLYING

THROUGHOUT THIS ACTIVITY BOOK, you have learned that the words you use (and the tone of voice you choose) really matter when it comes to bringing an end to bullying. In this Activity, you'll learn more than 50 encouraging words and phrases you can use to help others before, during, and after bullying.

THINK ABOUT IT

Have you ever seen someone else hurting, but not known what to say to help them feel better? This activity will help make sure you are never again at a loss for kind, encouraging words.

Directions:

On the next page, you will find a list of 50 Kind Words and Phrases. These are things you can say to someone before, during, or after they are bullied. (Or you can say them anytime a person needs a bit of kindness!) Read the whole list and circle the 10 words and phrases you are most likely to use.

50 KIND WORDS AND PHRASES

1. You are awesome.

2. Do you want to sit with me on the bus today?

3. Let's sit together at lunch.

4. I'll text you after school.

5. I know you can handle it.

6. You are strong.

7. You are a great friend.

8. I'm so sorry she said that to you. That wasn't right.

9. You didn't deserve her cruelty.

10. You've got this.

11. I understand.

12. I've been there.

13. Me too.

14. You handled that so well. I'm impressed!

15. I don't know if I could have done that as well as you did. Good job!

16. How did it go?

17. Let me know how it goes.

18. I know you'll do great.

19. Don't give up, no matter what.

20. I've got your back.

21. I'll be there for you no matter what.

22. Don't pay any attention to what they say.

23. You rock.

24. Is there anything I can do to help you?

25. Try not to take it personally.

26. Who cares what anyone else thinks? What matters is what you think!

27. Text me and let me know what happens.

28. I'll cross my fingers for you.

29. Good luck!

30. Do you need to talk?

31. I believe you.

32. I believe in you.

33. Believe in yourself!

34. I think you should tell a teacher about what just happened. If you want, I'll go with you.

35. Would you mind if I tell a teacher about what just happened?

36. How did you do that?

37. I'm excited to see what you do.

38. I know you're going to do great.

39. I like hanging out with you.

40. It's fun to do things with you.

41. I'm glad you're here.

42. I'm happy to talk with you.

43. Do you want to hang out after school?

44. I'll walk you home from the bus.

45. I'll meet you after class and go with you to your locker.

46. I'm listening.

47. I'm here for you.

48. You make me laugh.

49. You're the best.

50. You're my BFF.

WEEKLY LOG

Over the next 7 days, keep a record of the kind words and phrases you say to others. In the space provided, write down WHAT you said, WHY you said it, and HOW the other person responded.

EXAMPLE:

DAY I:

I said: _"I'll walk you home from the bus."_

Because: _A few kids in our neighborhood kept teasing Jenna on the bus._

He/ she: _Smiled at me and said, "Thank you!" She seemed relieved._

DAY 1:

I said: _____

Because: _____

He/she: _____

DAY 2:

I said: _____

Because: _____

He/she: _____

DAY 3:

I said: _____

Because: _____

He/she: _____

DAY 4:

I said: _____

Because: _____

He/she: _____

DAY 5:

I said: _____

Because: _____

He/she: _____

DAY 6:

I said: _____

Because: _____

He/she: _____

DAY 7:

I said: _____

Because: _____

He/she: _____

You're the best!

I'm with you.

You can do it

ACTIVITY 32: WHAT'S YOUR TAGLINE?

NOW THAT YOU HAVE completed Activities 29 to 31, you know that standing up for someone who is being bullied is:

1. Easy

Use any of the 10 Things to Say and Do to Stop Bullying (pages 167–168) to stand up for anyone you see being bullied.

2. Timeless

Anytime is a good time to reach out to a person who is being bullied. You can say or do something before, during, or after bullying to be a hero to someone who needs your help.

3. Kind

Look back on your Weekly Log (pages 179–181) to see how many people you can help by saying kind words. Words matter a lot! Your kind words will help a bullied person feel supported and less alone.

In this Activity, you will learn a fourth fact about standing up for those who are bullied. You will learn that these easy, timeless, and kind acts are:

4. Your responsibility!

Read on to find out more.

THINK ABOUT IT

Standing up for someone who is being bullied starts with you. Yes, YOU! You might be hoping a parent or teacher will do something about the problem. Or maybe you think someone who is better friends with the person being bullied will step in. Perhaps you are just crossing your fingers and hoping that the bullying stops on its own.

Forget any of these "Someone else will stop it" options!

If you know that bullying is happening to someone else, YOU have the power and the responsibility to do something to stop it.

So, what will you do to stop bullying anytime you are a witness to it?

Tell The World Your Tagline

Directions:

1. Come up with your own phrase (or borrow one below) that best describes your role in standing up for others. Examples of good taglines are:

- Be Known for Being Kind
- Stopping Bullying Starts with Me
- It Only Takes One
- Bullying Stops Here
- I M Here 4 U
- Keep Calm & Stop Bullying

2. Write down your tagline here: _____

3. On the next 2 pages, design a T-shirt that tells your bullying prevention tagline to everyone you meet. Be as creative as you'd like! Use color, designs, or even texture to make your tagline stand out!

EXAMPLE:

(FRONT)

(BACK)

YOUR DRAWING HERE:

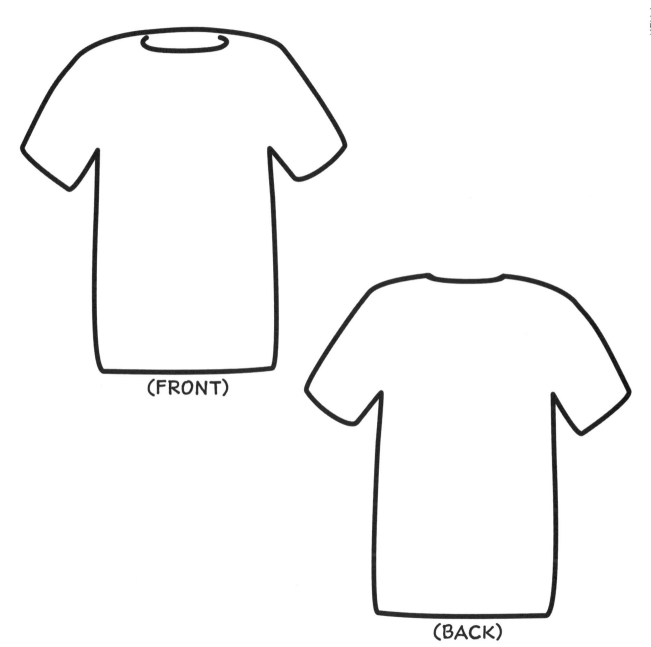

(FRONT)

(BACK)

Key 6: Be Known for Being Kind

CHECKPOINT

1. Mark **T** for True or **F** for False for each of these statements:

   _____ Bystanders are around during only 5 out of every 10 cases of bullying.

   _____ Kids stand up for those being bullied less than 2 times out of 10.

   _____ When kids do step in to stop bullying, it usually stops within 10 seconds.

2. Which of the following is NOT a helpful thing to say or do to stop bullying?

   a. Use a *Meek* voice
   b. Change the subject
   c. Show kindness
   d. Get help

3. Which of the following is a good time to stand up for someone who is being bullied?

   a. *Before* the bullying in order to prevent it
   b. *During* the bullying to stop it on the spot
   c. *After* the bullying to support and comfort the person
   d. All of the above

4. List 3 kind phrases you can see yourself saying to someone who has been bullied:

_____

_____

_____

5. Stopping bullying starts with you! (Circle the correct answer.)

True   **False**

Key 6: Be Known for Being Kind

☑ CHECKPOINT

A N S W E R   K E Y

1. Mark **T** for True or **F** for False for each of these statements:

_____F_____ Bystanders are around during only 5 out of every 10 cases of bullying.

_____T_____ Kids stand up for those being bullied less than 2 times out of 10.

_____T_____ When kids do step in to stop bullying, it usually stops within 10 seconds.

2. Which of the following is NOT a helpful thing to say or do to stop bullying? (Circle one.)

(a.) Use a *Meek* voice

b. Change the subject

c. Show kindness

d. Get help

3. Which of the following is a good time to stand up for someone who is being bullied?

a. Before the bullying in order to prevent it

b. During the bullying to stop it on the spot

c. After the bullying to support and comfort the person

(d.) All of the above

4. List 3 kind phrases you can see yourself saying to someone who has been bullied:

   Any kind phrases that sound natural are correct!

5. Stopping bullying starts with you! (Circle the correct answer.)

   (True)   **False**

KEY 6: *I am on my way to being known for being kind!*

REACH OUT TO KIDS WHO BULLY

ACTIVITY 33: EVERYONE HAS A STORY

IN THIS SECTION, you will be challenged to do something unexpected. Something different. Something that shows true kindness and compassion. You will read 2 real-life situations about bullying, but instead of being asked to use *Mean-It* words or to stand up for the person being bullied, you will be asked to think about *what might be going on in the life of the person doing the bullying.*

Making time to see from a new point of view is rare. Most people want to find the guilty person, punish him, and be done with it. And yet we know from Activity 28 that there are at least 2 sides to every story. In this Activity, you will learn that *every person has their own story.* Stopping bullying often starts with learning the whole story of each person.

THINK ABOUT IT

Read each situation below. Then use the space provided to answer questions about the story of the person who bullied.

Situation 1

What witnesses saw:

Jada and Liza were playing together at recess. They were laughing and skipping and chatting. All of a sudden, their classmate, Riley, ran up behind them. Riley grabbed one end of Liza's scarf and started pulling on it so that Liza turned around to face her. Then, quick as a flash, Riley grabbed the other end of Liza's scarf. She crossed it around Liza's neck and started to choke her! Liza was stunned. Jada called out for help. Two recess aides arrived and pulled Riley off Liza. Riley was sent to the Principal's office. Her parents were called to pick her up. She was suspended from school for 5 days.

Based on what the witnesses saw:

1. Who do you think acted like a bully? _____

2. Who do you believe was being bullied? _____

3. Do you think Riley's punishment was fair? _____

What most people didn't see:

For the last 4 school days, Jada and Liza had been taunting Riley. They had been making fun of her during class, at lunch, and during recess. Each day, they would make fun of the horse stickers on her notebook. They would taunt her about how food got stuck in her braces. At recess, they kept making promises to play with her, but then they would run away every time she got near them. On Friday,  Riley found out that Jada and Liza had been writing love notes to a boy named Ollie, pretending that they were written by Riley. Riley was embarrassed when all of Ollie's friends laughed in her face at recess.

Feeling hurt and angry, Riley tried to catch up with Liza to ask her what was going on with the notes. Riley kept calling Liza's name, but Liza did not turn around. To get Liza's attention, Riley ran up behind her and grabbed the end of her scarf to get her to turn around. Liza looked at her and said, "Oh, look! It's Ollie's girlfriend!" Jada laughed out loud. At that point, Riley got so mad that she grabbed the other end of Liza's scarf. Before she even knew what she was doing, she was pulling the ends around Liza's neck. The next thing she knew, 2 recess aides were screaming at her and she was being marched to the Principal's office.

Now that you know more of the story:

1. Who do you think acted like a bully? _____

2. Who do you believe was being bullied? _____

3. Do you think Riley's punishment was fair? _____

4. How did your point of view change when you learned the whole story?

_____

_____

_____

Situation 2

What witnesses saw:

Kyle was a quiet kid who usually kept to himself. But every time he got frustrated, he would take out his feelings on his classmates. One day, he couldn't understand the math lesson. He called the kid sitting next to him a "butt-face loser." Another day, a girl cut in front of him in the lunch line. He shoved her and knocked her tray to the floor. Her food spilled everywhere. Last week during gym, Kyle felt embarrassed about being picked last. He punched one of the team captains right in the stomach.

On Wednesday, Kyle arrived late to school. His clothing was wrinkled and his hair smelled funny. He fell asleep during language arts. When his teacher went to wake him, he yelled, "Get off me, you stupid witch!" and swatted her arm. When the girl next to him laughed, Kyle kicked her desk over and yelled, "What are you laughing at, you ugly butt-face?" Kyle was sent out of class and told to go straight to the counselor's office.

Based on what the witnesses saw:

1. Who do you think acted like a bully? _____

2. Who do you believe was being bullied? _____

3. What do you think should happen to Kyle? _____

What most people didn't see:

By the time he was in 3rd grade, Kyle had already lived in 7 foster homes. His mother was in prison. He had never met his dad. This month, Kyle was living in a house with 2 other foster children. One of them was a 14-year-old boy named Christopher. Christopher was really mean to Kyle. He always took Kyle's clothes and food. He called Kyle names like "butt-face loser." Worst of all, when he got mad, he would hit Kyle and kick his things. On Tuesday night, Kyle played video games until 3 a.m. He was trying to stay awake to make sure that Christopher didn't steal any more of his things. Kyle finally fell asleep in his clothes. He woke up the next morning too late to shower, change, or even eat breakfast before school.

Now that you know more of the story:

1. Who do you think acted like a bully? _____

2. Who do you believe was being bullied? _____

3. What do you think should happen to Kyle? _____

4. How did your point of view change when you learned the whole story?

_____

_____

_____

MORE TO THINK ABOUT

It can be scary to watch bullying happen—especially in school where all kids deserve to feel safe. To be clear: **There is no excuse for violence. There is never a time when name-calling is okay.** The purpose of this Activity is not to excuse Riley, Kyle, or any kids who hurt others. But it is important to know that _what you see with your eyes is not all there is to see._

In any situation, it is good to slow down and get information about a situation before you decide what is going on. Show that you are smart by finding out what happened _before_ the bullying you saw. Share your kindness by understanding that there may be more to the situation than meets the eye.

Sometimes, you will find that the event was as simple as one person being cruel to someone else. Other times you will learn that there was a long chain of events that led up to the bullying you saw. The person who appeared guilty at first might actually be a victim of cruelty.

KEY POINT

It is important to take time to understand a person and his situation. Only then can you respond well.

WRITE ABOUT IT

Has anyone ever punished you for something they thought you did, without understanding the full story of why you did it? Describe the event:

- What did others see you do?
- What else was happening that these people did not know about?
- What did you learn?

✎ _____

_____

_____

_____

_____

_____

_____

_____

_____

_____

_____

_____

Remember, it is never okay to be cruel or violent. It is important to keep in mind that every person has a story. This is a first step in ending conflict and solving problems.

ACTIVITY 34: 5 FAVORITE THINGS ABOUT ME

CAN YOU NAME YOUR 5 FAVORITE MOVIES? What are the 5 flavors of ice cream you'd like to have in your freezer at all times? Are there 5 famous cities you'd like to visit?

In this activity, you'll create a **5 Favorites** list of the things you love most about yourself. You will learn how celebrating yourself can help bring an end to bullying.

THINK ABOUT IT

What could a **5 Favorites** list of things you love about yourself have to do with stopping bullying? Before moving on, write down your answer to this question in the space below:

_____

_____

As you learned way back in Activity 1, kids who bully are often trying to build up their own **P**ower. Feeling powerful can be a great thing. But when kids build themselves up by pushing others down, it's like a real-life game of Whack-a-Mole that has no winners!

One of the best ways to bring an end to bullying is to take so much pride in yourself and have so much confidence in your abilities that no one can push you down.

Some kids worry that taking pride in themselves is like bragging. The 2 things are definitely different! Use this simple chart to know the differences between taking pride in yourself and bragging to others:

TAKING **PRIDE** OR **BRAGGING**?

YOU ARE TAKING **PRIDE** IN YOURSELF IF:	YOU ARE **BRAGGING** IF:
You talk about trying hard and being the best you can be. **Example:** *I practiced for an hour every single night to learn that song on the piano. I'm so happy the hard work paid off.*	You talk about how easy it is to be so much better than other people. **Example:** *I barely practiced at all and I still did better than anyone else at the piano recital.*
You encourage yourself and others at the same time. **Example:** *Our team was awesome today! There was so much good passing and scoring by all of us.*	You lift yourself up by pushing others down. **Example:** *Did you see how many times Jonny fumbled the ball? It's his fault we didn't get that touchdown. Good thing I was there to score the winning touchdown!*
You celebrate your own strengths. **Example:** *Art is my best subject.*	You compare yourself to others. **Example:** *I'm the best artist in the whole school.*

Now you understand how pride is different from bragging. You know that being proud of who you are can even protect you from the effects of bullying. It's time to get started on your **5 Favorites** list!

Directions:

On page 201, write down 5 of the best things about you. The only catch is, you are **NOT** allowed to list items related only to how you look. So, for example, you should **AVOID** writing down something like:

> **1.** I love my long legs.

> **OR**

> **2.** My red hair is so fabulous.

On the other hand, you **CAN** list how your body helps you do something or how a trait makes you unique, such as:

> **1.** I love that my long legs help me to run very fast.

> **OR**

> **2.** I feel special that I am the only person with red hair in my whole grade.

KEY POINT

Try your best to focus your **5 Favorites** list on your inner qualities—traits like kindness, loyalty, and being a good listener. These are the traits that help you connect with others. They help you become even stronger in the face of bullying.

5 **FAVORITE** THINGS ABOUT ME

1. _____

2. _____

3. _____

4. _____

5. _____

CONGRATULATIONS on completing your **5 Favorites** list. But wait; you are not done yet!

Building self-confidence does not happen overnight. Writing down 5 things you love about yourself *today* will not help you unless you read the list *tomorrow*—and the *next day*—and the *day after that* . . . and so on. Staying strong in the face of bullying is not a single event, but rather an everyday activity. Your **5 Favorites** list is meant to be just the beginning.

To take this activity to the next level, try at least one of these Bonus Challenges:

1. Use a phone to film yourself reading your **5 Favorites** list aloud. This video is not to be posted online or viewed by anyone else. This recording is simply for you—to watch every day to remind you of your best qualities. Watch it whenever you need an extra boost of confidence.

2. Read the list aloud to a parent, brother, sister, or other relative. It may feel embarrassing at first, but hearing their comments on your strengths can help boost your pride and confidence even more. Maybe you'll even inspire someone you love to create their own **5 Favorites** list!

3. Repeat the **5 Favorites** list aloud while looking in the mirror. Do this each day for the next 10 days. You will likely feel awkward at first. By Days 8, 9, and 10, though, you may notice that your words feel more true and your strengths are real. You may realize that you are far too confident to let anyone else bring you down.

ACTIVITY 35: I AM WHO I AM!

IN THE LAST ACTIVITY, you learned to take pride in what makes you strong and unique. In this Activity, you will create a piece of word art that says even more about makes *you* wonderfully *you*.

THINK ABOUT IT

> Most of us are many different things, to many different people. Whether or not we like acting on stage, we all play several roles in life. There is no one in the world exactly like you. This is your chance to celebrate that wonderful fact!

Directions:

Using the large "I" on the next page, create a work of art. Fill the space inside the "I" with words, phrases, emojis, or even pictures. They should describe the roles you play, the people you love, the subjects that interest you, and anything else that describes your unique place in the world.

An example is provided to help you get started thinking about the possibilities for your "I Am" masterpiece!

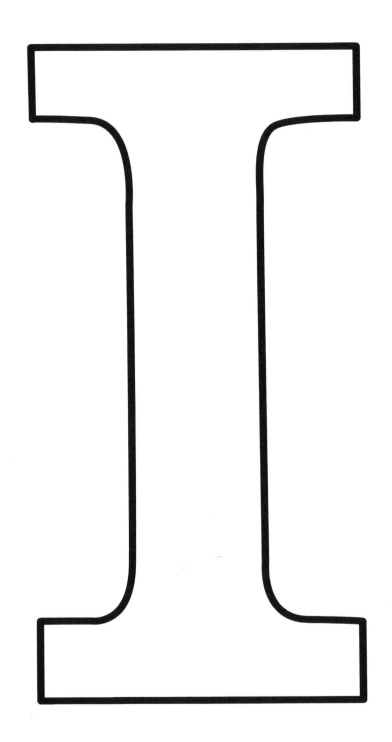

ACTIVITY 36: QUIZ TIME: WOULD YOU RATHER?

WOULD YOU RATHER HANG OUT with a person who is "popular" at school or with someone who is "well-liked" by most people? In this Activity, you'll play the "Would You Rather" game. This will help you find out what is most important to you when it comes to choosing your friends.

THINK ABOUT IT

- What is the difference between being "popular" and being "well-liked?" Write down a few words to describe each in the space below:

  "Popular" means: _____   _____   _____

  "Well-liked" means: _____   _____   _____

- If you had to choose, would you rather be part of a popular crowd at school or be well-liked by most people? (Circle one.)

  Popular   **Well-liked**

- Is it possible to be both popular AND well-liked? Explain in your own words how a person can be BOTH at the same time:

  _____

  _____

  _____

Now it's time to have some fun. Play the **Would You Rather** game on the next page. Read some of the real-life choices kids your age face when it comes to forming friendships. You will learn about your own style for deciding what matters most in a friend.

Would You Rather . . .

Directions:

Using any color pencil or crayon, shade the choice you are most likely to make in each of the 12 situations.

1. Play a game you like with kids who are not very nice to you.	Or	Play a game you don't like with kids who are always nice to you.
2. Be the first person picked for the team.	Or	Be the first person a friend turns to when they need to talk.
3. Be invited to every classmate's birthday party this year but not hang out with any of them at school.	Or	Spend time at school each day with 2 close friends but not be invited to any other birthday parties.
4. Swim in a pool full of M&M's.	Or	Swim in a pool full of Skittles.
5. Hang out with someone who is really fun and exciting but not very kind.	Or	Hang out with someone who is really kind but also a bit boring.
6. Win a $25 gift certificate to an ice cream shop and go with a kid who is mean to everyone.	Or	Spend $5 of your own money to go out for ice cream with your best friend.

7. Be the oldest kid in your family.	Or	Be the youngest kid in your family.
8. Be known for being beautiful.	Or	Be known for being kind.
9. Play with a classmate who wears stylish clothes but insults your outfits.	Or	Play with a classmate who has no sense of style but is really adventurous and fun.
10. Hang out with a kid who owns all of your favorite video games but never lets you have a turn to play.	Or	Hang out with a kid who only owns 3 games but always makes sure you get a fair amount of time to play.
11. Be able to fly.	Or	Be able to make yourself invisible.
12. Have a friend that is nice to you in person but says mean things online.	Or	Have a friend that posts really nice things about you online but is mean to you in person.

MORE TO THINK ABOUT

Look back on your responses to the **Would You Rather** game.

IF YOU CIRCLED THE ITEMS ON THE LEFT MOST TIMES:

It is clear that being popular is important to you. You are not alone in wanting to fit in with the crowd and "be known" by all the kids. It's OK to enjoy being popular, but make sure that you don't climb your way to the top of the social ladder by pushing anyone else down. Be known for being kind always—to everyone, and not just the kids who sit at the cool table or who are invited to all the parties. Make sure that the kids you spend time with treat you well. These kids should ask you what you think, include you when they talk, respect your choices, and help you feel good about yourself whenever you are together.

IF YOU CIRCLED THE ITEMS ON THE RIGHT MOST TIMES:

You have the strength and confidence to value real friendships. It is important to you to have a few close friends that you can be yourself with. You know that it might be fun to go to a few more birthday parties. It could be cool to brag that you own all the latest video games. But you know that spending time with kids who are always kind and trustworthy is a whole lot better. Have faith in your choices. Whenever you are able to choose your friends, *choose kind.*

IF YOU CIRCLED ANY ANSWER FOR #4, #7, OR #11:

You are correct! These **Would You Rather** questions were thrown in just for fun. So, M&M's or Skittles—which will it be?

IF YOU CIRCLED EITHER ANSWER FOR #12:

This question is the hardest choice of them all. Neither answer sounds very good, does it? As you learned in Activities 14 to 20, technology can make friendships complicated! Whenever you can, *refuse to choose* between options like the ones in #12.

A friend is someone who is kind to you in person AND online. You should never have to make a choice between the two. If you find that a kid acts one way online and a totally different way in person, it's time to use your skills from Activities 12 and 13 to tell this person how you feel about what they are doing. If the person keeps treating you badly, use your skills from Activity 26 to move away from this friendship with dignity.

KEY POINT

It's not always easy to make smart choices when it comes to friendships. Sometimes your heart tells you one thing while your brain tells you another. The great thing about a game like **Would You Rather** is that the consequences of your choices are pretty clear: Either spend time with kids who are popular but not very nice in person, or spend time with someone you can count on to be kind and fun most of the time. Which type of friendship *would you rather* enjoy?

Activity 37: Staying Tuned In to Others

ARE YOU BUSY? Do you ever feel like you spend most of your day rushing from home to school, to the bus, to after-school activities, to practices, to games, to friends' houses, to get homework done, and to brush your teeth before bed—all just to start the same rush the next day? Many of us lead very busy lives. It's easy to see how sometimes we get so busy taking care of ourselves that we forget to notice the feelings and needs of those around us. This fun (and tasty!) Activity* will help you keep others in mind, even when there's a lot going on in your own life.

THINK ABOUT IT

Being able to understand and share in the feelings of others is called **empathy**. The skill of empathy allows you to know how someone else is thinking and feeling because you have been through something like it in your own life. In other words, empathy helps you put yourself in someone else's shoes and see from their point of view.

When you show empathy to someone who has been bullied, you help them to feel less alone and more understood. When you show empathy for a person who has acted like a bully, as in the examples in Activity 33, you can help them understand that there are different, better choices that can be made for acting out their troubles.

This next activity gives you a great way to understand the idea of empathy. It will help you to show empathy anytime you find out about a bullying situation.

* Linda Van Voorst, "Ice & Marshmallow" activity, www.justicekids.org. Used with permission

Sweet Empathy

Directions:

For this activity, you will need:

- A handful of small, sweet treats, such as mini marshmallows or M&M's
- A few ice cubes

Step 1:

Eat 2 to 3 of the sweet treats. Savor the flavor. Then, in the space below, write down a few words to describe their taste and texture (such as *sweet*, *smooth*, or *soft*).

_____   _____   _____

Step 2:

- Now, place an ice cube in your mouth. Keep the ice cube on your tongue for as long as you can—until either it melts or your mouth is so cold that you can't take it anymore.
- As soon as the ice cube is gone, place 2 to 3 of the sweet treats in your mouth. Quickly, write down words to describe their flavor now:

_____   _____   _____

Step 3:

Did you notice a difference in the taste of the sweets before and after eating the ice cube? Circle the answer that best describes what happened AFTER eating the ice:

    a. The sweet treats tasted the same the second time around.

    b. The sweet treats tasted even sweeter the second time around.

    c. I couldn't taste the sweets treats as well the second time around.

Discussion

- In Step 1, it should have been easy to taste the flavor of the sweet treats.
- In Step 2, however, you held the ice cube in your mouth for a while. Your tongue became frozen, or *numb*. When your tongue is numb, your sense of taste does not work for a while.
- For that reason, in Step 3 most people choose answer C: "I couldn't taste the sweets treats as well the second time around."

This is how it is with bullying!

Sometimes we get so caught up in our own busy lives or in our own thoughts and feelings that we become *numb*. Our ability to sense the feelings of others doesn't work as well for a while. One of the best ways to bring an end to bullying is to always stay tuned in to the feelings of others—both kids who are bullied and kids who bully others. When you show empathy for what is happening to others, you help them to feel better understood, less alone, and more able to make good choices in how they treat others.

Key 7: Reach Out to Kids Who Bully

CHECKPOINT

1. Stopping bullying starts with: (Circle the best answer.)

a. understanding that there are 2 sides to every story.

b. asking a kid who was not involved what he saw and taking his word for it.

c. getting revenge to teach the bad kid a lesson.

d. acting like it's no big deal when kids are cruel to each other.

2. Next to each sentence, write down if it is an example of TAKING PRIDE or BRAGGING.

a. _____ No one is as good at soccer as I am!

b. _____ I'm proud of how I did on my math test.

c. _____ Ella can't dance. I'm way better than her.

3. Circle **True** or **False** for the following statements:

a. One reason to take pride in yourself is because the things you like about yourself can help you connect with others and make you feel stronger in the face of bullying.

True   False

b. Everyone agrees that it is better to be popular than to be well-liked.

True   False

4. Empathy is: (Circle the best definition.)

a. feeling numb to how others are feeling.

b. not really caring about what other people are thinking.

c. the ability to understand and share in the feelings of others.

d. the ability to get everyone in the room to do what you tell them.

Key 7: Reach Out to Kids Who Bully

CHECKPOINT

A N S W E R   K E Y

1. Stopping bullying starts with: (Circle the best answer.)

    (a.) understanding that there are 2 sides to every story.

    b. asking a kid who was not involved what he saw and taking his word for it.

    c. getting revenge to teach the bad kid a lesson.

    d. acting like it's no big deal when kids are cruel to each other.

2. Next to each sentence, write down if it is an example of TAKING PRIDE or BRAGGING.

    a. _BRAGGING_   No one is as good at soccer as I am!

    b. _TAKING PRIDE_   I'm proud of how I did on my math test.

    c. _BRAGGING_   Ella can't dance. I'm way better than her.

3. Circle **True** or **False** for the following statements:

    a. One reason to take pride in yourself is because the things you like about yourself can help you connect with others and make you feel stronger in the face of bullying.

    (True)   **False**

    b. Everyone agrees that it is better to be popular than to be well-liked.

    True   (False)

4. Empathy is: (Circle the best definition.)

    a. feeling numb to how others are feeling.

    b. not really caring about what other people are thinking.

    (c.) the ability to understand and share in the feelings of others.

    d. the ability to get everyone in the room to do what you tell them.

KEY 7: *I know how to reach out to kids who bully!*

KEEP TALKING ABOUT ENDING BULLYING!

ACTIVITY 38: KINDNESS MATTERS

LITTLE ACTS OF KINDNESS make a big difference in stopping bullying. Sometimes, they make the biggest difference of all. In this Activity, you will learn the power of one word, one smile, one door held open, one invitation to sit together at lunch, one text just to say "hi," or one high-five offered each and every day.

THINK ABOUT IT

Has a compliment from a friend ever brightened your rough day? Has a nod from your teacher ever given you the confidence to keep trying? Neither of those *actions* took a lot of time or cost money, but both are the types of kindness that can turn someone's whole day around. When young people make kindness cool, bullying won't stand a chance at school!

Kindness Challenge

Directions:

1. Using the worksheet on the next page, read the 20 ideas for simple, quick, and no-cost acts of kindness that you can do for others at school or at home.

2. Select 1 act of kindness from the worksheet. Your challenge is to carry out this kindness AT LEAST ONCE PER DAY, OVER THE NEXT 30 DAYS.

3. Whenever you can, carry out the act of kindness for a DIFFERENT PERSON each day. Spread as much kindness as possible!

4. Record your acts of kindness in the 30-DAY KINDNESS CHALLENGE LOG on page 215.

KINDNESS CHALLENGE
What will you do to make someone's day?

1. Look someone in the eye and smile.

2. Make a thank-you card for a service man or woman.

3. Help make dinner for your family.

6. If you see someone sitting alone at lunch, at recess, or on the bus, invite them to sit with you.

. Give a high-five a teammate. Tell hem they made a great play.

5. Clean up your room without being asked.

10. Let someone go in front of you in line.

7. Compliment a classmate.

8. Donate clothes and books that you don't use anymore.

9. Offer to do a sibling's chore.

12. Tell a parent something you appreciate about them.

11. Say hello to someone you don't usually talk to.

14. Thank a teacher for something new that they taught you.

15. Leave a kind note in a library book for the next reader to find.

13. Write an anonymous note of encouragement to a classmate.

16. Tell a joke to make a classmate laugh.

18. Clean up a mess in the classroom without being asked.

17. Set the table for dinner.

19. Hold a door open for someone.

20. Text a friend just to say "hi" and see how their day is going.

DRAW A PICTURE OF YOURSELF CARRYING OUT
1 (OR MORE!) OF THE ACTS OF KINDNESS LISTED
ON P. 219. BE SURE TO SHOW HOW YOUR ACT OF
KINDNESS MAKES SOMEONE ELSE FEEL!

30-DAY KINDNESS CHALLENGE LOG

Record your act of kindness and who you did it for in the space provided.

If you see the person's reaction to your kindness, please note it.

✿ DAY 1	✿ DAY 2	✿ DAY 3	✿ DAY 4	✿ DAY 5	✿ DAY 6
✿ DAY 7	✿ DAY 8	✿ DAY 9	✿ DAY 10	✿ DAY 11	✿ DAY 12

✿ DAY 13	✿ DAY 14	✿ DAY 15	✿ DAY 16	✿ DAY 17	✿ DAY 18
✿ DAY 19	✿ DAY 20	✿ DAY 21	✿ DAY 22	✿ DAY 23	✿ DAY 24
✿ DAY 25	✿ DAY 26	✿ DAY 27	✿ DAY 28	✿ DAY 29	✿ DAY 30

IN ADDITION to choosing 1 act of kindness to perform each day over the next 30 days, make it a goal to *carry out all 30 of the acts of kindness listed.* Color in each shape as you complete it.

When the entire **KINDNESS CHALLENGE** worksheet is colored, carefully tear out the page from your Activity Book. Proudly display it in your room, on the fridge, or anywhere you will see it. It will remind you that your 30 simple acts of kindness made a big difference to others.

ACTIVITY 39: CREATE-A-CAMPAIGN

HAVE YOU EVER THOUGHT about what you would do if you were in charge of your school? Being the Principal would be too big a job for a kid, but what if you could run the bullying prevention activities for the year?

This Activity lets you create your own Bullying Prevention Campaign at school. It includes making a schedule of events, activities, projects, and games that you think would be helpful in bringing an end to bullying and building better friendships among kids.

THINK ABOUT IT

October is National Bullying Prevention Month in the United States. During these 31 days, many schools and other places for kids have activities to raise awareness for ending bullying. You know how important it is to keep kids safe throughout the year. Your mission is to create a *Bullying Prevention Campaign* that lasts throughout the school year. In the space provided, plan fun activities that teach bullying prevention messages all year long.

To get you started, here is a list of common bullying prevention activities hosted by schools. Use any of these—or come up with your own ideas—to involve students and teachers in efforts to end bullying throughout the year.

COMMON BULLYING PREVENTION ACTIVITIES

- Poster contests
- T-shirt days
- Assemblies
- Author visits
- Film festivals
- Mix-it-up lunches
- Book fairs
- Walks
- Pledges

On the next few pages, plan at least one **Bullying Prevention Campaign** event for each month of the school year. Think about the main goal of your event, how many students and teachers you will need to help you make it happen, a list of supplies, and any other important details. Let your imagination run wild! Dream big. Be creative. **It is up to you to create the change that you want to see in the world.**

EXAMPLE (BASED ON ACTIVITY 38):

ACTIVITY NAME:	The **30-Day Kindness Challenge**
GOAL OF ACTIVITY:	To show that little acts of kindness make a big difference in stopping bullying
WHAT WILL HAPPEN:	Kids will think of no-cost, simple acts of kindness. They will choose 1 act to carry out each day of the month and record their **30 Acts of Kindness** in a journal.
WHO WILL HELP PLAN:	One student from each grade, along with 2 teachers to help organize students and tell the whole school about the Challenge
SUPPLIES NEEDED:	Each student completing the Challenge will need their own journal to record the Acts of Kindness for 30 days.
OTHER DETAILS:	Kids will share their journals with their teacher and classmates at the end of the 30 days.

BULLYING PREVENTION CAMPAIGN

MONTH 1

ACTIVITY NAME: _____

GOAL OF ACTIVITY: _____

WHAT WILL HAPPEN: _____

WHO WILL HELP PLAN: _____

SUPPLIES NEEDED: _____

OTHER DETAILS: _____

_____

MONTH 2

ACTIVITY NAME: _____

GOAL OF ACTIVITY: _____

WHAT WILL HAPPEN: _____

WHO WILL HELP PLAN: _____

SUPPLIES NEEDED: _____

OTHER DETAILS: _____

_____

MONTH 3

ACTIVITY NAME: _____

GOAL OF ACTIVITY: _____

WHAT WILL HAPPEN: _____

WHO WILL HELP PLAN: _____

SUPPLIES NEEDED: _____

OTHER DETAILS: _____

_____

BULLYING PREVENTION CAMPAIGN

MONTH 4

ACTIVITY NAME: _____
GOAL OF ACTIVITY: _____
WHAT WILL HAPPEN: _____
WHO WILL HELP PLAN: _____
SUPPLIES NEEDED: _____
OTHER DETAILS: _____
_____

MONTH 5

ACTIVITY NAME: _____
GOAL OF ACTIVITY: _____
WHAT WILL HAPPEN: _____
WHO WILL HELP PLAN: _____
SUPPLIES NEEDED: _____
OTHER DETAILS: _____
_____

MONTH 6

ACTIVITY NAME: _____
GOAL OF ACTIVITY: _____
WHAT WILL HAPPEN: _____
WHO WILL HELP PLAN: _____
SUPPLIES NEEDED: _____
OTHER DETAILS: _____
_____

BULLYING PREVENTION CAMPAIGN

MONTH 7

ACTIVITY NAME: _____

GOAL OF ACTIVITY: _____

WHAT WILL HAPPEN: _____

WHO WILL HELP PLAN: _____

SUPPLIES NEEDED: _____

OTHER DETAILS: _____

_____

MONTH 8

ACTIVITY NAME: _____

GOAL OF ACTIVITY: _____

WHAT WILL HAPPEN: _____

WHO WILL HELP PLAN: _____

SUPPLIES NEEDED: _____

OTHER DETAILS: _____

_____

MONTH 9

ACTIVITY NAME: _____

GOAL OF ACTIVITY: _____

WHAT WILL HAPPEN: _____

WHO WILL HELP PLAN: _____

SUPPLIES NEEDED: _____

OTHER DETAILS: _____

_____

ACTIVITY 40: WHAT'S YOUR VIDEO MESSAGE?

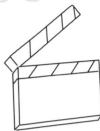

CONGRATULATIONS on reaching the last part of your Activity Book! Through the first 39 Activities, you have gained all kinds of smarts and skills for ending bullying. *You are now stronger, wiser, and more able to help yourself and others.* In this last Activity, you'll make your own video to share some of what you have learned.

THINK ABOUT IT

Think back on your favorite activities from this book:
- Which worksheets helped you learn something new?
- Was there a quiz that you found especially fun?
- Did the information about your amazing brain amaze you?
- Have you started using *Mean-It* phrases already?
- Did the ideas for standing up for others before, during, and after bullying help you help someone else?

IN THE SPACE BELOW, WRITE DOWN 3 OF THE ACTIVITIES YOU REMEMBER MOST:

1. _____
2. _____
3. _____

One focus in this Activity Book was on the many ways that you can use technology to have fun and be creative. In this final activity, you are challenged to do just that!

Directions:

Create your own 2- to 3-minute video that features strong, kind ways that young people can make a difference in their school, their neighborhood, or even their country to bring an end to bullying. Be creative. You may choose to highlight a piece of learning from any of the activities in this book, or you may choose to feature your own ideas. This is your chance to use your powerful voice to spread positive messages about stopping bullying.

After you have created your original video message, share it with your parents, teachers, family, and friends. The more widely you share your message, the more people will learn about helpful ways to bring an end to bullying.

WITH PERMISSION FROM A PARENT, consider sending your video message to me by email at signe@signewhitson.com. Selected videos will be posted to the *8 Keys to End Bullying Activity Book* channel on YouTube. Tune in to watch video messages posted by other kids your age. Just remember: Only positive, encouraging comments are permitted on our channel! Kindness matters in person, online, and everywhere you go. Our community is a safe place for kids to share their messages about bringing an end to bullying.

Good luck creating your video message! I hope to see it on YouTube!

Key 8: Keep Talking About Ending Bullying!

CHECKPOINT

1. _____ acts of kindness make a _____ difference in stopping bullying. (Circle the best answer.)

    a. Big, little

    b. Little, big

    c. Cold, hot

    d. Hot, cold

2. When young people make kindness cool, bullying

    _____!

    (Fill in the blank. HINT: The answer can be found in Activity 38!)

3. Which month is National Bullying Prevention Month in the United States?

    a. September

    b. October

    c. November

    d. December

4. Name at least 3 common bullying prevention activities that take place in schools:

_____   _____   _____

5. If you had to name the single most important idea or new skill you learned in this Activity Book, it would be:

_____

Key 8: Keep Talking About Ending Bullying!

 CHECKPOINT

ANSWER KEY

1. _____ acts of kindness make a _____ difference in stopping bullying. (Circle the best answer.)

    a. Big, little

    (**b.**) Little, big

    c. Cold, hot

    d. Hot, cold

2. When young people make kindness cool, bullying
   Won't stand a chance at school !

3. Which month is National Bullying Prevention Month in the United States?

    a. September

    (**b.**) October

    c. November

    d. December

4. Name at least 3 common bullying prevention activities that take place in schools:

Any of the following responses are correct. You may even have different events at your school. Those are correct responses also!

- Poster contests
- Author visits
- Book fairs

- T-shirt days
- Film festivals
- Walks

- Assemblies
- Mix-it-up lunches
- Pledges

5. If you had to name the single most important idea or new skill you learned in this Activity Book, it would be:

_____

Whatever you wrote is the correct answer for you. Use your new ideas and skills to help yourself and others whenever you can!

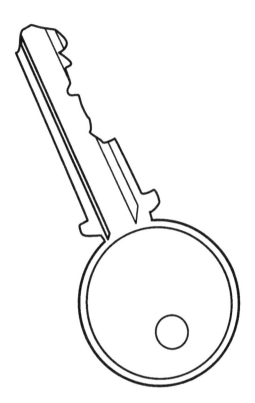

KEY 8: *I won't stop talking about ending bullying!*

A FINAL NOTE

Dear Readers,

Congratulations! Completing the activities in this book is a sign of your strength, your smarts, and your hard work to bring an end to bullying. By reading, writing, and thinking about better ways to handle conflict, you are bringing about change in your world.

 As with kindness, it is the little things you do each day that make a big difference in how people treat one another. *Always remember the importance of a smile in the hallway, a friendly hello, a text to say "hi," or a hug to make someone feel valued.* Thank you for putting in the time, thought, and effort to make all of our days a little kinder and a lot more fun.

 There is a *Certificate of Achievement* on the next page. This is an award for your efforts to manage bullying with kindness and compassion. Your next challenge is to make sure that this is not the *end* of your Activity Book, but the *beginning* of the end of bullying. Make it happen. You WILL make a difference!

With admiration and respect,

CERTIFICATE *of* ACHIEVEMENT

THIS ACKNOWLEDGES THAT

[Recipient Name]

HAS SUCCESSFULLY COMPLETED THE

8 KEYS TO END BULLYING
ACTIVITY BOOK

[MONTH DAY]
[YEAR]

Anonymous: In an *anonymous* report, you can tell a trustworthy adult what happened in a bullying situation without saying your own name. It can be helpful to stay *anonymous* if you want to be honest without having someone get mad at you, take revenge, or call you a tattletale.

Bully: The word *bully* should always be used as a verb. *To bully* someone is to hurt them on purpose, over and over again, using an imbalance of power. The word *bully* should not be used as a noun to refer to a specific person. It should not be used as an adjective to describe a young person's personality. Every kid makes mistakes. Every kid deserves to be taught better ways to behave. No kid should be labeled a bully.

Bullying: *Bullying* is cruel behavior done on purpose, repeated over time, that involves an imbalance of power. To understand bullying, remember the 3 **P**'s:

1. It is done on **P**urpose. There is nothing "accidental" or unplanned about bullying.

2. It is a **P**attern. The cruelty happens over and over again.

3. It is all about **P**ower. The cruel person has more control and influence than his or her target.

Bystander: A *bystander* is someone who is present while bullying is taking place or knows that bullying is happening to someone. You have the power to make a positive difference in someone's life by stepping in to stop bullying and standing up for victims of bullying. This is called being a hero, an ally, and a helpful *bystander*.

Confidential: In a *confidential* bullying report, a trustworthy adult protects your safety by not saying that you were the one who gave information. You can always talk to an adult about bullying and ask him or her not to use your name.

Cyberbullying: *Cyberbullying* is a kind of bullying that involves technology, such as cell phones, computers, social media, apps, or gaming systems. Cyberbullying can be really harmful because of how quickly and how far cruel messages can spread.

Emotional Skills: *Emotional skills* have to do with a person's ability to manage strong feelings such as anger, frustration, sadness, confusion, and fear. Conflict and bullying often create strong feelings in kids. Key 5 shows you how to build strong social and *emotional skills* so that you can handle bullying well.

Empathy: *Empathy* is the ability to understand and share in the feelings of others. The skill of *empathy* helps you see from someone else's point of view.

Mean: A person who is *mean* says or does something on purpose to hurt someone else. Unlike bullying, mean behavior usually happens only once or twice. It often occurs between people who are usually friends. If not stopped, however, mean behavior can turn into bullying.

Netiquette: *Netiquette* is a word created by combining the words *Internet* and *etiquette*. *Etiquette* is another word for manners. *Netiquette* is a set of rules for using the Internet and other technology (such as cell phones, apps, social media, tablets, or gaming devices) in ways that are polite and respectful.

Numb: The word *numb* refers to a loss of feeling. In Activity 37, the ice cubes freeze a person's tongue so that it becomes *numb.* For a short time, it can't feel or taste the sweetness of food.

Physical bullying: *Physical bullying* happens when one person tries to harm another person's body. Some of the most common kinds of *physical bullying* are hitting, kicking, hair pulling, pushing, and spitting.

Pledge: A *pledge* is a promise to follow certain rules.

Relational bullying: In *relational bullying*, kids use relationships to hurt others. One of the most common kinds of *relational bullying* is threats to take friendship away ("I won't be your friend anymore if . . ."). Other kinds are the silent treatment, getting people to gang up on someone, and leaving someone out on purpose. Because *relational bullying* often happens between friends who used to trust each other, it can be very confusing and hurtful.

Rude: A person who is *rude* says or does something by accident that hurts someone else. Examples of *rude* behavior are butting in line, burping without saying "Excuse me," and bragging about being the smartest kid in school. Rudeness usually isn't planned.

Social Skills: *Social skills* have to do with a person's ability to get along with others and form positive friendships. People with good *social skills* show empathy and care for others, handle change well, and make good choices. Key 5 shows you how to build strong emotional and *social skills*, which will help you handle bullying.

Tattling: *Tattling* is when a kid tells an adult about another kid's behavior in order to get the person in trouble.

Telling: *Telling* is when a kid tells an adult about something that happened because they are trying to get help for someone who is hurt or can't solve an important problem on their own. In a *telling* situation, the main goal is to keep a person safe.

Verbal Bullying: *Verbal bullying* is using words to hurt others. Some of the most common kinds are, taunting, calling names, and threatening. Some people say that "words will never hurt you," but anyone who has received *verbal bullying* knows that cruel words can be very painful.

Victim: A *victim* is a person who is harmed by someone else. A person who gets bullied may be called a *victim* or a target. Please note that not all victims are weak or defeated. Many people who are victims of bullying learn new skills. This can help them to become stronger and more powerful than ever!

JUST FOR YOU

These Just for You! pages are a place for you to journal, draw, and collect your thoughts. You can use them to work through challenging situations. You can also celebrate the times when you handle conflicts really well! Making notes about what works (and what doesn't!) is a great way to keep track of the best ways to bring an end to bullying anytime it happens.

DRAW A PICTURE OF A BULLYING SITUATION THAT HAD A DIFFICULT ENDING

DRAW A PICTURE OF A BULLYING SITUATION THAT YOU HANDLED WELL

JUST FOR YOU

_____

_____

_____

_____

_____

_____

_____

_____

_____

_____

_____

_____

_____

_____

_____

_____

JUST FOR YOU

JUST FOR YOU

_____

_____

_____

_____

_____

_____

_____

_____

_____

_____

_____

_____

_____

_____

_____

_____

_____